MOTORIZED BICYCLES:

FROM MOTORBIKES TO MOPEDS TO EBIKES

Tom Bartlett

First published in 2010

Copyright © 2010 by Tom Bartlett

All rights reserved. With the exception of quoting brief passages for the purposes of review, no part of this book may be reproduced without prior written permission from the publisher.

This publication is not approved or licensed by any of the manufacturers mentioned within. We recognize that some words, model names, and designations mentioned herein are the property of the trademark holder. We use them for identification purposes only. This is not an official publication.

ISBN 978-0-557-64369-1   Printed in the United States of America

Some of the many placements of motorized bicycle engines

#1: Dayton, Singer. #2: Velosolex, Bike Bug, Ohlsson & Rice, Aqua Bug. #3. Harley, Excelsior, Whizzer, Zipcycle. #4: DynaCycle, Cucciolo #5: Cyc-Auto, Villiers Junior, New Hudson, James, Puch, Peugeot Bima, Mobylette #6: Johnson, Cyc-Aid. #7: Merkel, Wall, Smith, Briggs. # 8: Indian.

Foreword

I think the idea must have occurred to the majority of bicycle riders at one time or another—the idea to put a motor on their bike. Mostly, I suspect the idea occurred while pedaling up a long incline or on a particularly hot and humid day. I am aware that a significant percentage of cyclists ride for physical exercise or to remain in shape or for the sheer fun of it, and so they are not interested in such a system, but they won't be reading this book anyway.

What I am sure of is that the idea of motorizing a bicycle occurred early after the invention of a practical bicycle and occurred often and continues unabated to this very day. My research into the history of motorizing the bicycle left me amazed at the proliferation of patents and the number of attempts at manufacturing a workable engine for a bicycle. And not to leave out my own efforts, I have included a chapter of the history of my involvement with the manufacture of motorized bicycles. Had I been more aware of the number of failed start-ups, I am sure I would have been more cautious about my investment of time and money.

But that is jumping ahead in the story. This book grew out of my interest and love for bicycling in every form from classic pre- and post-war bikes to sleek aluminum mountain bikes to bicycles with sidecars to tandems to recumbents to motorized bikes to collecting obscure bicycle motors. My garage looks like a small unorganized motorized bicycle museum and I would not part with any of them. I have thoroughly enjoyed building, riding, re-building, and repairing my motorized bikes. My bookshelves are overflowing with books about bicycles and motorcycles, but missing are any serious treatments of the wide field of motorized bicycles. So I wrote this book to try to fill some of the gaps. After all, the motorcycle industry really started with the idea of putting an engine on a bicycle.

And as the book will reveal, innovation and invention have not abated, but seems to continue at an even faster pace. Today, it is possible to purchase an engine kit to motorize your bicycle on the Internet and be riding it after a weekend of wrenching. I can vouch for the process and I have friends who have accomplished the same and were out riding their motorized bike the next weekend.

Table of Contents

Chapter 1	The Early History of Bicycles and Engines	1
Chapter 2	Add-On Engines and Motor Wheels	13
Chapter 3	European Autocycles and Cyclemotors	23
Chapter 4	The Whizzer Story	29
Chapter 5	The American Scene from the 50s to the 70s	41
Chapter 6	Millions of Mopeds	49
Chapter 7	The Zen of Zipcycle	55
Chapter 8	Roll Your Own	65
Chapter 9	The Import Explosion of Engines from China	71
Chapter 10	The Electric Powered Bicycle	77
Appendix	Motorized Bicycle Clubs and Forums	84

1869 Roper Steam Powered Bicycle

1892 Millet Steamer

Chapter One

The Early History of Bicycles and Internal Combustion Engine

In the beginning, they were all motorized bicycles. The modern motorcycle was the result of the merging of two developments in the late 1800s, the bicycle and the internal combustion engine. Both of these advances had their roots in the industrial revolution that was occurring in the late 1700s and early 1800s. The need for power more portable than a watermill or more constant than a windmill drove innovators to seek any method of providing power for the new machinery being invented. In Europe, a different kind of revolution was brewing. Internal combustion engines had existed, at least in theory, with the design of a gunpowder engine of Huygens and Papin in England in the early 1700s. But the new revolution involved a race to perfect a power source of any type, be it gas or steam or electrical. Some of the best and brightest minds in the world were hard at work at nights, on weekends, in solitary and in teams.

An important prerequisite to the development of internal combustion (or external combustion, such as steam engines, for that matter) was the adoption of a system of patent laws that allowed inventors to profit from their efforts and reap the benefits, if any were coming. The earliest system of granting patents seems to date from about 1474 when they were introduced in Venice. From there a similar system spread to England where the first patents were granted in 1552. The English system was codified and spread to Scotland in 1707. The English patent system provided the basis for the American system, which was passed in 1790 and the first administrator was the Secretary of State, Thomas Jefferson. The French adopted a system of patent laws in 1791, but

German (or the Prussian States) lagged until about 1842. In 1887 the U.S. joined the Paris Convention and granted reciprocal recognition of European patents. The patent system, with all its flaws, still was a major inducement to technological progress during and after the industrial revolution.

Most historians trace the invention of the bicycle back to the "running machine" of Baron Karl Von Drais, a German Forest Master who invented it to help him cover the territory within his job requirements. About 1813 Von Drais first tried a mechanical four-wheeled vehicle in which two riders supplied the arm power for propulsion. This proved to be unwieldy, so in 1817 he unveiled his improvement, which was a two-wheeled cycle with a steerable front wheel and was straddled and pushed by the feet. Von Drais called his invention a "laufmaschine", or running machine. It was wider known under the name "Draisene" after Von Drais' own name and then later became known as a "velocipede" or Latin for "fast foot." Von Drais demonstrated how the rider could alternately push with each foot and travel three or four yards with each push. Plus, after gaining the top of a hill, the rider could then coast all the way down the other side and partly up the next hill. For the first time, riders had to learn how to balance a two-wheeled vehicle. Von Drais proved that a person could travel a much greater distance each day riding his velocipede and arrive less tired because the rider's weight was mostly carried by the wheels. The two-wheeler quickly caught on in Europe, particularly in England and France, where the beginnings of good roads were being developed. Because Germany had not yet developed a patent system, Von Drais was allowed to retire from civil service and still receive a pension in reward for his inventions. He also invented an early typewriter and a wood-saving cooker.

The Von Drais "laufmaschine" or running machine

Von Drais' two-wheeler became known as the "hobby horse" or the "dandy horse" because of the young men who quickly adopted this latest fashion. Although the new fad spread widely, even to America, it remained roughly the same until about the 1860s when a new development broke open the floodgates of innovation and improvement.

The new development seems to have begun in France, where some innovator added a set of pedals to the front wheel. The actual inventor is still subject to some controversy, since two individuals, Pierre Michaux and Pierre Lallement, both claimed to have originally conceived the idea. Michaux became more successful because of his manufacturing prowess and promotional abilities. Michaux had a successful blacksmithing business and began building bicycles with pedals on the front wheels in the 1860s. Pierre Lallement, on the other hand, was building baby carriages in the 1860s and declared that he was the one that added the vital pedals to a hobby horse. Later Lallement immigrated to the United States where he successfully patented his improvements. He was unable to interest any investors in his invention so he returned to Paris, where Michaux and his son were successfully building the pedal bicycles. Some bicycle historians credit Lallement rather than Michaux for the initial invention; however Michaux was a far better promoter of his products.

Michaux Velocipede. This one is very early. Note that the classic "diamond frame" had not yet evolved.

Nevertheless, this innovation started a revolution in human-powered transport. From this beginning, improvements came rapidly. Bicycle frames became lighter and stronger. Advances were made in many different areas. The first iron frames appeared, constructed by rolling tubes from sheets of iron. These frames could be highly decorated with paint and scroll-work. The wheels were still being made of wooden rims with iron hoops but builders later switched from wooden spokes to strong, light-weight steel spokes with solid rubber tires. These first bicycles with solid rubber tires became known as "Bone Shakers" because of their stiff ride over cobblestone streets. Precision ball bearings began to appear on the more expensive bicycles.

But for the next twenty years of so the development of the bicycle took a detour that did not lead to adoption by a wide populace. The problem was in the proper gearing for the drive wheel. The first bicycles were driven by pedals affixed to the front wheel, so to increase speed the only avenue was to increase the size of the front wheel. Although these larger wheels gave a much smoother and faster ride, the front wheels continued to grow larger—so large that the resulting machine, though fast, was tricky to ride and dangerous to riders. Known as the "High Wheeler", the light-weight bicycles set new distance and speed records almost monthly. The first tubing frames appeared on the high wheelers, along with early precision ball bearings. But riders were in constant danger of being catapulted over the large front wheel. Braking was especially dangerous and going downhill presented a challenge every time. The high-wheelers were a dead-end in development of the bicycle.

The classic high wheeler required a brave rider— some might say foolhardy.

A major development in 1885 breathed new life into the development of the bicycle. In this year, Joseph Starley of England introduced his "safety" bicycle, one that had two wheels of about the same size, but was chain-driven by the rear wheel with the rider sitting much lower than with the high wheeler. This radical innovation completed the development of the bicycle, for it allowed the proper gearing for the rear wheel and at the same time was controllable and safe to ride. The rider sat lower and in no danger of being catapulted over a front wheel. With the improvements in pneumatic tires offered by Scotsman John Boyd Dunlop and Frenchman Andre Michelin, distance and speed records soon outclassed the achievements of the high wheeler. Within 10 years the "high-wheeler" ceased to be manufactured as they were replaced by variations of Starley's safety bicycle. Starley's design was widely copied and became the de facto standard for the bicycle wheel layout.

When Starley hit upon the idea of driving the rear wheel by means of a sprocket and chain, the modern bicycle was born.

But almost as soon as a workable bicycle appeared, inventors in both the United States and Europe quickly began efforts to motorize it. In Paris in 1868, the bicycle manufacturer Pierre Michaux had commissioned L.G. Perreaux to design and construct a steam engine to drive one of Michaux's "boneshaker" bicycles. The engine that Perreaux designed had a single brass-plated steel cylinder, a lightweight steel piston rod, and a tube-type boiler. The engine, which sat underneath the seat, burned alcohol fuel and exhausted its fumes by means of two pipes down low behind the rider. The rider, who had to be a brave fellow, started the cycle by foot pedals on the front wheel, and once forward motion and balance was established, opened the valves to allow pressurized steam into the cylinders.

The Perreaux-Michaux Steam Driven Bicycle of 1868. Note that the rider is sitting directly over the steam boiler.

At about the same time an American, Sylvester Roper, was building a steam-powered bicycle in 1869. Roper's steam-powered bicycle made its first public appearance on this date in his hometown of Roxbury, Massachusetts. His invention delighted the public and Roper spent the next few years touring fairs and gatherings in New England demonstrating his hickory-framed two-wheeler. Roper was a skilled machinist and inveterate inventor who brought out his versions of sewing machines, guns, machine tools, furnaces, automatic fire escapes and eventually steam-powered carriages and bicycles.

In 1895, with backing from the Pope Manufacturing Company, Roper built an improved version of his steamer bike. Pope foresaw the possibility of adding new business to his bicycle empire. In 1896, when he was in his 70s, Roper felt he had his steamer bike perfected. He was demonstrating his speed at the Charles River bicycle racetrack in Boston when he crashed. It was later determined that Roper had died of heart failure. Today, the Smithsonian displays his original steam bicycle.

The Roper Steam Powered Bicycle did not use a chain; the twin pistons drove the rear wheel by the connecting rods.

Meanwhile in 1884, Arizona engineer Lucius Day Copeland combined a Starr high-wheeled bicycle driven by levers attached to a small steam engine, with the result being a steam powered motorcycle. The steam engine developed about 1/4 hp and had the boiler and gasoline heater built around the steering column. A flat leather belt drove the large rear wheel. Copeland's invention appeared several times throughout the United States but seems never to have been put into production.

However, the immediately available power that could be obtained from a gasoline internal combustion engine began to overshadow all steam engine developments. The first patent for a gas (coal-derived gas in the form of vapor, not liquid petroleum) engine had been filed in Britain as early as 1794 and some gas engines were produced for pumping water out of mine shafts. But liquid fuels derived from petrol began to take the place of gas derived from coal. The problem with piped-in gas was that the customer and factory had to be located within a mile or so of the works where the coal gas was manufactured. Liquid fuels derived from petroleum, on the other hand, were easily stored and transported.

A method had to be developed to ignite the mixture of gas and air so the first petroleum engines were ignited by an externally-heated hot tube. The first engines to be ignited by electrical means were the ones built by Karl Benz. The first really successful high-speed petroleum engine was the work of Nicholas Otto in Germany in the early 1870s. Although many of the large Otto engines were sold and put into use to drive industrial machinery, the first light-weight liquid gas engine was designed and built by Gottleib Daimler and Paul Maybach in 1885. To make this new engine operate successfully Daimler and Maybach had to invent a carburetor that mixed the petrol with air.

The Daimler-Maybach high-speed, light weight petrol engine became the forerunner of virtually all motorcycle and automobile engines.

To test their new engine, they installed it in a wooden-framed and wheeled motorcycle-type vehicle. Daimler and Maybach had no plans to put their motorized cycle into production, but used it as a test bed for their new engine. Installed into a two-wheeled vehicle and called the "Einspur", or "single track", their vehicle was to go down in history as the world's first internal combustion powered vehicle, even if it did have two small wheels on each side of the rear to help balance it. The two small added wheels looked exactly like our modern training wheels on Junior's bicycle. The wooden-framed bicycle that they built in the summer of 1885 followed the design of James Starley's "safety bicycle" which had just been put into production in Coventry, England and utilized two main wheels of about the same size. It was also the only motorcycle they ever made.

Daimler and Maybach felt the small side wheels were necessary because neither of them had ever ridden a bicycle.

This period was just before the introduction of the pneumatic tire by John Dunlop (in 1888), so Daimler and Maybach shod their machine in iron bands around the spoked wooden wheels. Since neither Daimler nor Maybach had any experience in riding or balancing one of the new-fangled bicycles, Daimler's 16-year old son, Paul, volunteered to become their test driver. In the fall of 1885 Paul rode their new invention three kilometers to the next town and returned safely still under power. He wrote out a short summary, possibly the world's first drive test report. His younger brother Adolf, aged 14, also tried out the machine and reported that the hot exhaust opening just underneath the seat made for a hot ride. This may have been the world's first critical drive report.

As winter was coming in, Daimler modified the motorcycle into a sort of motorized sled with runners in the front, but his partner Maybach persuaded him to put the improved engine in a special-built carriage. This motorized carriage was the beginning of a long line of automobiles manufactured by Daimler-Benz and much later they brought out a lighter and more powerful sports-car that was named the Mercedes.

A mention here needs to be made of what is normally deemed to be the "world's first motorcycle", mainly because (1) It was a motorcycle that actually went into production, and (2) It used a specially-built frame, not a bicycle frame. The motorcycle is generally referred to as the Hildebrand-Wulfmuller motorcycle, and it was first produced in 1894. The Hildebrand brothers, Heinrich and Wilhelm, had a background in making steam engines before they turned their attention to gasoline engines.

1894 Hildebrand & Wulfmuller motorcycle. Most historians of the early motorcycle feel that this may be the earliest motorcycle that was put into production. Note the connecting rods drive the rear wheel, not a chain.

They obtained backing from Alois Wolfmuller to build their design for an internal combustion driven motorcycle. It was a water-cooled twin cylinder four-stroke engine of 1488cc. Drive was by connecting rods to the rear wheel. In 1894 they registered the term "motorrad" which was German for "motorcycle", the same year the vehicle was patented. Built in Germany and France from 1894 to 1897, these are the world's first production motorcycles. The "motorrad" used the newly-developed Dunlop pneumatic tires.

But the rest of the early pioneers of motorcycling got their start mostly by first manufacturing bicycles and then motorizing them. George M. Hendee (1866 - 1943) was a teen-age sensation as a bicycle racer, winning the United States National Amateur High Wheel Championship in 1886 and setting a speed record that was not broken until 1892. Hendee was America's first national cycling champion and retired from active bicycle racing in 1892 to enter the bicycle manufacturing business.

George Hendee's first business was making bicycles in Springfield, MA

After a couple of unsuccessful attempts at partnerships, he set up his own company in 1898 and named his new brand of bicycles "Indian". Hendee also promoted and sponsored bicycle races to advertise his products. While attending a bicycle race at Madison Square Garden in 1900, Hendee watched the speed and smoothness of a motorized pacing bicycle built specially to start bicycle races. A few inquiries led Hendee to the builder of the motorized pacer, Oscar Hedstrom (1871 - 1960).

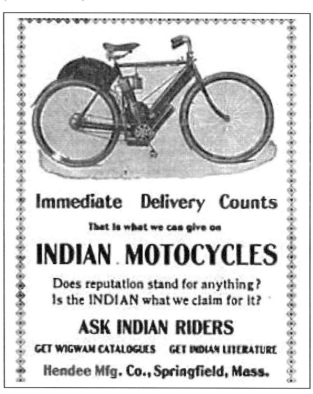

For the first five years Hendee referred to his motorized bicycles as "Motocycles" in his ads.

Hedstrom was a journeyman engineer who had designed and cast his own engines which had proven to be more reliable and powerful than the competition. Hendee and Hedstrom became partners in 1901 and began work on a motorized bicycle to be known as an Indian. With Hedstrom closely supervising all aspects of the manufacturing, the pair developed a sophisticated and sound

1904 Excelsior (American)

The 1903 and 1904 Indian Motocycles carried their gasoline supply in a tank placed over the rear wheel, hence the nickname "Camelback". Note also that the engine becomes a load-bearing part of the seat down tube. They were all pedal started.

motorized bicycle. Just as Hendee had gotten his start in competition of bicycle races, the company also competed in motorcycle races and the Indian gained an early reputation for winning. After building three examples in 1901, the next year they build and sold 143. All the early Indians were pedal-started bicycles with the addition of a motor. In 1903, Hedstrom set the world motorcycle speed record of 56 miles per hour. From there the Indian went from success to success. Hedstrom brought out a V-twin engine in 1907 and the days of motorizing a bicycle were numbered because of the increasing power of the engine. In 1909 Indian abandoned the bicycle frame and went to a strengthened motorcycle-type frame. But motorizing bicycles had given the pair their start in the motorcycle business.

William S. Harley and his school friend Arthur Davidson began experimenting with internal combustion engines about the turn of the century. Harley worked as a draftsman and Davidson worked as a pattern maker. In 1903 they built a 400cc single cylinder engine and installed it in a bicycle. It worked well but the need for more power was apparent, so Harley added more power by increasing the size to 475cc.

Is this one of the first Harley-Davidson Ads? It appeared in the February 1905 issue of <u>Automobile and Cycle Trade Journal</u> (p. 453).

In 1904 the Harley-Davidson Motor Company began production of "The Silent Gray Fellow." All of the companies' motorcycles were started by pedaling the bicycle and letting out the clutch. If the engine failed for any reason while on a trip, the vehicle could still be pedaled like a bicycle, just not very fast.

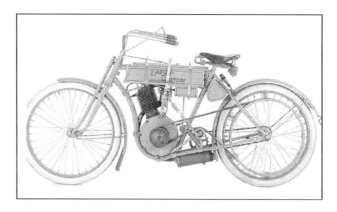

1906 Harley-Davidson single, still pedal started with leather belt drive.

In 1907 Harley-Davidson built their first v-twin, but it was still pedal started. In fact, Harley-Davidson maintained the pedal-start feature on all their motorcycles through the year 1915. The motorcycles were started in one of two ways; either by pedaling the cycle (preferably downhill if possible), or by lowering the rear wheel stand (which jacked the rear wheel into the air) and pedaling away until the engine started. Then the rider climbed off (with the engine still running) and pushed the cycle forward and rotated the wheel stand up into the traveling position by positioning it in the catch on the rear fender. But by 1915 their engines had grown so large and powerful that they were difficult to pedal start by either manner, so after this year they developed a geared-kick starter that was much easier to operate.

In a similar manner, the Excelsior brand motorcycle company got its start in 1876 as a bicycle manufacturer called the "Excelsior Supply Company" in Chicago Illinois. Their first motor driven cycle was built in 1909 and had a single-cylinder engine with a leather belt-drive with a top speed of around 40 miles per hour. In 1912 the Schwinn Bicycle Company purchased the Excelsior Company and continued producing motorcycles under the same name, but the early ones were all pedal-started.

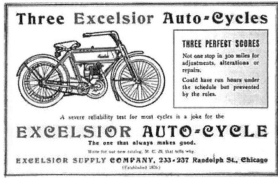

P. Lallement's American Connection

Pierre Lallement seems to have seen the future but was unable to get anyone to listen. Born in Nancy, France in 1843, he moved to Paris as a young man and began working just as the bicycle was being invented. Lallement went to his grave proclaiming that he was the true inventor of the bicycle and there are many who believe his claims. He left France in 1865 and came to the U.S., settling near Ansonia, CT. He applied for and was granted a patent for a velocipede:

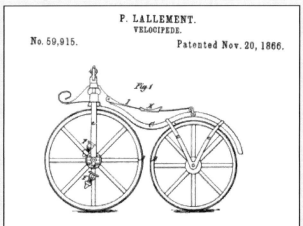

This is the earliest reference to a bicycle in the United States record. Lallement was never able to find backers for his invention so he sold the patent rights to Col. Albert Pope. He went back to Paris in 1868 to find the velocipede in volume production.

Lallement returned to the U.S. in 1880 and began working for the Pope Manufacturing Company. He died in obscurity in 1891 in Boston, MA at the age of 47. Lallement was inducted into the United States Bicycling Hall of Fame in 2005.

CHAPTER 1

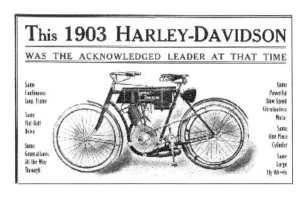

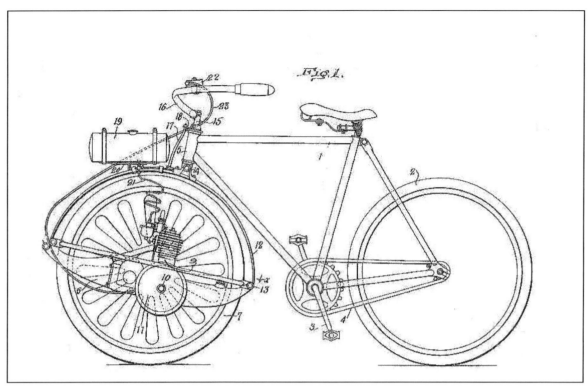

The Patent for the Dayton Motor Bicycle. It was powered by a Smith Motor Wheel fitted to the front.

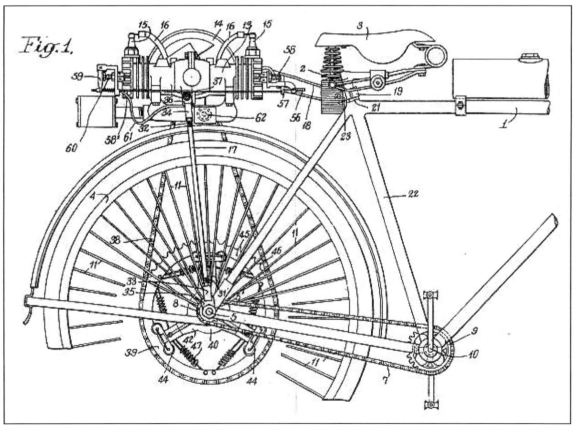

The patent for the Johnson Twin Cylinder Motor Wheel. It was fitted to the rear wheel. This engine later became the basis for the highly successful Johnson Light Twin Outboard motor.

Chapter Two

Bicycle Add-On Engines and Motor Wheels

Some of the very first producers of motorized bicycles sought to leave the bicycle's basic character unaltered and attempted to build add-on engines that could be fitted afterward to a regular bicycle by most owners with average abilities. They wished to take advantage of the huge numbers of bicycles already on the roads and byways. One of the first of these was a team of motor engineers from Coventry, England, Frank Birch and his partner, Edwin Perks. In 1899 they announced and demonstrated a motorized wheel for bicycles. In short, they were able to enclose a four-stroke engine within two aluminum wheel halves and power the wheel itself. The wheel then could replace the front wheel of a standard bicycle or even a tricycle. Although they built and sold a few examples of their Birch and Perks "Power Wheel", the design rights were quickly purchased by the Singer Bicycle Company also of Coventry. Singer put the motor wheel into production, mainly for their own bicycles and tricycles, but also offered the motor wheel alone for others to add to their bicycles. The first Singer Motorwheel caused a sensation when it was exhibited at the 1901 International Motorcar Exhibition in London. Singer went on to adapt and improve upon the original design to produce a more conventional motorcycle and powered three-wheeler. The company was successful and began a long history that progressed from powered bicycles to motorcycles to three-wheelers to four wheeled automobiles.

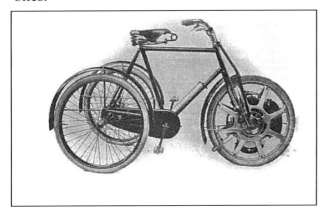

Since the Singer Motor Wheel could fit on the front, it made an ideal attachment for a tricycle

In the United States, Stanley Shaw of Galesburg, KS built his own steam engine in 1895, but soon switched to gasoline engines and perfected his first one in 1902. In 1905 he was granted a patent for his small air-cooled gasoline engine, one that would be a perfect fit to power a bicycle. Shaw advertised his engine in national magazines for years. The Shaw engine customer could purchase a complete motor ready to run, a kit to assemble, or rough casting kit to machine and assemble on their own. Reportedly through the years over 13,000 kits were sold, either in finished or unfinished versions. Shaw later produced a complete automobile and a kit that transformed a Ford Model T into a tractor. But he got his start building engines for motorized bikes.

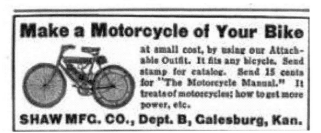

The Wall Motor Wheel was a separate wheel that fastened to the right rear side of the bicycle.

The earliest innovator to successfully build and market an aftermarket engine for the thousands of regular bicycles on the road, at least in Europe, must have been Arthur William Wall of Birmingham, England. By the early 1900s England alone had over 300,000 bicycles and Wall wanted to tap into this enormous customer base. Wall was an entrepreneur who had already developed an early motorcycle called the ROC, but in 1909 he entered a patent for an add-on motorized third wheel that bolted on the side of the rear wheel of a regular bicycle and provided power. A prolific inventor with multiple patents, Wall devised a motorized wheel to attach to the side of a bicycle with clamps. Others were busy motorizing bicycles, but Wall's invention did not require any alteration in the bicycle. Wall went through three iterations before he finalized his design, but each version was an improvement over the earlier. The final version was a vertical one horsepower four-stroke engine with an overhead inlet valve and a side exhaust valve. Approximately 10,000 were sold over the next few years, including some that were marketed by BSA as the BSA Auto

Wheel Deluxe. The engine drove a spoked 20 inch bicycle wheel by means of a reduction chain.

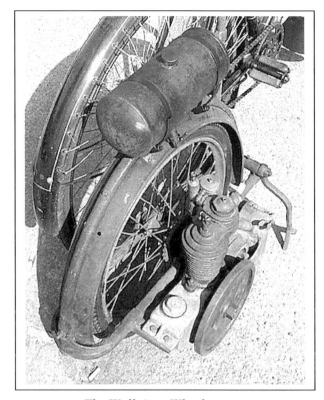

The Wall Auto Wheel top view

Wall was not the only one who saw opportunities in the large number of bicycles on the roads. Much later someone would coin the term "aftermarket" for those who built accessories for the vehicles already on the road. An aftermarket supplier would describe Lloyd Raymond "Ray" Smith of Milwaukee, WI. Smith was the son of A.O. Smith, the founder of a large steel fabrication company in Milwaukee. A.O. Smith specialized in forming metal tubing such as that used in the manufacture of bicycles. In fact, before the turn of the century, the A.O. Smith Company was the largest producer of bicycle parts in the world. In 1911, L.R. Smith was vacationing in London when he observed the large number Wall Auto Wheels on the streets there. Naturally this would have caught his attention, so Ray Smith looked up the man behind all these devices. After some negotiations with Wall, Smith obtained the American rights to manufacture Wall's motor wheels. When he returned to Milwaukee, Smith had several Wall Auto Wheels in his steamer trunk.

L.R. Smith and the A.O. Smith engineers closely examined the Auto Wheels from a mass production standpoint. The Wall four-cycle engine itself was a proven design, but in order to provide the necessary speed reduction between the engine and the wheel, the engine employed a camshaft-driven sprocket and a chain reduction. The A.O. Smith team simplified this gear reduction method by adding more lobes to the camshaft, thereby slowing it down, and driving the wheel directly from the end of an extended camshaft. This method eliminated the drive system between the engine and wheel, namely the cam chain sprocket, the chain, and the wheel sprocket.

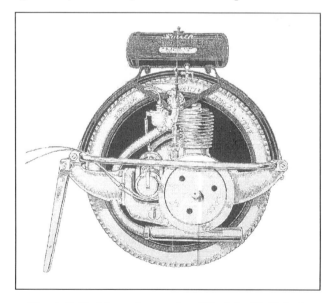

The A.O. Smith engineers simplified the Wall design by eliminating the chain and driving the wheel directly from an extension on the camshaft.

This change resulted in changing the rotation of the output, so the Smith engineers moved the engine from the original left side over to the right side, thus providing the proper rotation. To mount the engine, the team again went for a simpler method. Instead mounting the engine by tubing and brackets, they simply added two frame "horn" extensions made of cast aluminum that bolted on the side of the aluminum crankcase. This provided a much simpler and faster to assemble mounting system. The overall result of the changes by the A.O. Smith team led to an engine that was more economical to manufacture with less parts to possibly fail.

The Smith Motor Wheel could be attached to virtually any type or gender of bicycle.

American production of the Smith Motor Wheel began in 1914. A.O. Smith's position as a major supplier to bicycle companies gave the Motor Wheel a wide introduction. The first year sales were encouraging, so for 1915 the only thing changed was the addition of the words "Smith Motor Wheel" embossed on the flywheel. In 1916 sales of the Motor Wheel passed 10,000 and the company expanded its advertising efforts and began to distribute a magazine devoted to the uses for the motor wheel. Changes in1916 included a larger crankcase for a greater oil supply and a glass insert in the crankcase for the driver to visually check the oil level.

The company was always on the lookout for applications for the motorwheel; some that were adopted included powering a light-weight railroad inspection car that could easily be lifted off the tracks if needed and pulling a sled over frozen lakes in the winter.

The Motor Wheel was used as a power source for the Smith Flyer.

But the most popular application was to push a small light-weight wooden framed buckboard car. Named the "Smith Flyer", the little vehicle delighted all who saw it and years later gained the dubious honor of a listing in the Guinness Book of World Records as "The Most Inexpensive Car Ever Built". That is, if your definition of a car is a vehicle with four wheels, two seats, and a motor.

In 1988 A.O. Smith and his son L.R. Smith were the first father and son duo to be inducted into the Automotive Hall of Fame, along with their Smith Flyer.

By 1919 the A.O. Smith Company had sold over 25,000 motor wheels and flyers, but was being overwhelmed by orders, especially from the Ford Motor Company, for automobile frames. So the Smith Company made the decision to sell all the manufacturing rights to the motor wheel and flyer to the fledgling Briggs & Stratton Company, also of Milwaukee. Briggs & Stratton, also a successful manufacturer of automobile parts, wished to look into the manufacturing of small engines and saw the purchase as an opportunity to obtain the rights to an engine that had been thoroughly tested. Briggs & Stratton continued the production of the motor wheel and the flyer, but like the A.O. Smith Company, made more simplifying changes to the motor wheel.

Briggs moved the magneto inside the flywheel thereby simplifying the engine.

Stephen Briggs eliminated the outside gear-driven magneto and incorporated it into the flywheel, making the engine more reliable and also cheaper to manufacture.

He also increased the piston bore diameter, resulting in more power. Later, Briggs took the engine off the motor wheel and made it a "stand-alone" engine. This was easily done because the frame "horns" were simply bolted to the crankcase and the engine already had a gas tank.

Briggs then began to develop applications for his "portable" engine. He used it first to power a garden cultivator, then shortly afterward a generator, and then a water pump. As sales continued they later applied the little engine to a washing machine and to a lawn mower. Sales of the portable engines climbed so much that they had to build a new enlarged factory just to house the engine division. Years later, Briggs developed a lightweight aluminum block that became the standard for lawn mowers. Briggs & Stratton became the largest small engine manufacturer in the world and it all started from the motor wheel.

The Briggs bicycle engine became the ancestor of all subsequent Briggs & Stratton engines.

The Singer Company was not the only sewing machine company to convert to engines for bicycles. Take the Davis Sewing Machine Company of Dayton, OH, for an example. The company was originally founded in Watertown NY to produce sewing machines, but later moved to Dayton, OH and was headed by George Huffman. As a sewing machine manufacturer, the Davis Company not only had a cast iron foundry but also precision metal working machinery. As the bicycle business boomed in the 1890s, Huffman guided the company into adding a line of bicycles alongside their sewing machines. This proved to be a shrewd move and when the sale of sewing machines declined, the company prospered with a line of Dayton bicycles.

In 1915 George H. Gorman, a Dayton, OH, inventor, widened the front fork of a Dayton bicycle and installed a Smith Motor wheel to drive the front wheel. When Huffman saw the result he negotiated for the patent rights and began to produce a complete motorized bicycle.

The resulting Dayton Motor Bicycle was advertised as the "World's Lowest Priced Complete Motor Vehicle--$100.00". The company was careful not to advertise their product as a motorcycle, but rather a ready-to-ride motor bicycle, for the motorcycle field was already becoming crowed. George Huffman's son, Horace, founded the Huffman Manufacturing Company in Dayton in 1924 that would later become known as the bicycle giant Huffy. But it all started with sewing machines and motorized bicycles.

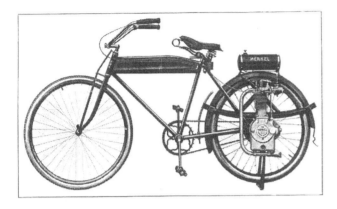

The Merkel Motor Attachment kit on a bicycle

At about the same time as Harley-Davidson and George Hendee of Indian were experimenting with putting engines on bicycles, Joseph Merkel of Milwaukee, WI was also developing a motorized bicycle. As a young man Merkel had apprenticed in a machine shop and learned the particulars of making machined parts that were light and durable. The practical mechanical experience gained in machining gave him a desire to learn more. He enrolled at Michigan Agricultural College (now Michigan State University) to study mechanical engineering. In 1897, Merkel accepted a draftsman position at E.P. Allis Co. (later to become Allis-Chalmers Co.) in Milwaukee. By the turn of the century, Merkel had opened his own business that manufactured bicycle parts. By 1901, Merkel was attaching small motors to bicycles and the Merkel Motorcycle was born. A motor-powered tricycle Merkel had built in 1900 was thought to be one of the first self-propelled vehicles built in Wisconsin. Merkel went on to build some of the most powerful and successful motorcycles in the United States, but he got his start building motorized bicycles.

In 1916 Merkel filed a patent application for a motor wheel attachment for bicycles. Merkel's approach was an advanced four-stroke overhead valve engine that mounted on a frame suspended from the rear fender of a standard bicycle. Instead of using a chain (like the Wall Auto Wheel) or an offset drive (like the Smith Motor Wheel), Merkel's design provided for a direct gear drive which drove the rear wheel. Merkel's kit included the engine, his especially adapted rear wheel, a gas tank and all the controls. But Merkel had made the decision to have the engine sub-contracted out to the Hendee Manufacturing Company of Springfield, MA, the manufacturer of the Indian Motorcycle. In the end Merkel's profit margins were too low and the company was forced into bankruptcy in 1918. All the assets of the Merkel Motor Wheel were purchased by the Hendee Manufacturing Company, which used the engines on their Indian bicycles.

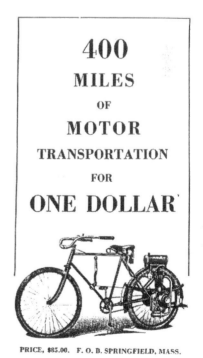

About the same time that Joseph Merkel was developing his motor wheel accessory, another group of engine builders were considering jumping into the already crowded bicycle engine business. The Johnson Brothers of South Bend, IN, had specialized in building large two-stroke marine engines when one of the brothers, Louis Johnson, applied for a patent for a twin cylinder bicycle engine in 1916. The engine, an innovative two-stroke horizontally opposed engine, was to be installed over the rear tire of an ordinary bicycle. Marketed as the Johnson Motor Wheel, the engine was compact and very light. The engine kit came with a rear wheel unit consisting of wheel, tire, sprocket and chain, a three quart gas tank and all the necessary fittings to adapt the engine and rear wheel unit to any standard 26" bicycle.

as a portable power unit for water pumps during World War I. And unlike the other motor wheel which was invented in England and transferred to the United States, the Johnson Motor Wheel design reversed the process, for it was produced under license in England by Victory Motors of Eynsford, Kent and marketed as the "Economic Bicycle Engine." The Johnson Motor Wheel quickly became a best seller, accounting for over 17,000 units sold over the next few years.

The Johnson twin opposed cylinders were supposed to provide a smoother power source than a single cylinder.

The engine proved to be sturdy and reliable, so much so that it was used by the U.S. Army

The twin cylinder bicycle motor made an excellent light outboard engine when adapted to a marine configuration.

By 1922 sales began to dwindle, so the Johnson Brothers searched for another application for their proven engine. They modified the flat twins to drive a small outboard motor. By switching to water cooling and adding a rope-start, the little engine made an ideal light outboard engine. The Johnson Outboard was introduced at the New York Boat Show in 1922 and was an immediate hit with 3,300 sales in the first year alone. For the next ten years the Johnson Brothers Outboards were industry leaders, but the Depression caught the company unprepared for the long economic slow down. Without sufficient capital the company was forced into bankruptcy in 1932 and the assets were purchased by Stephen Briggs and Ralph Evinrude. The separate companies Johnson, Evinrude, and Elto were folded into a new corporation entitled the Outboard Marine Corporation (OMC). Like so many others before them, the resulting companies owed their start to the humble bicycle engine.

1939 Cyc-Auto with Scott engine. In 1934 a similar motorized bicycle started the Autocycle saga.

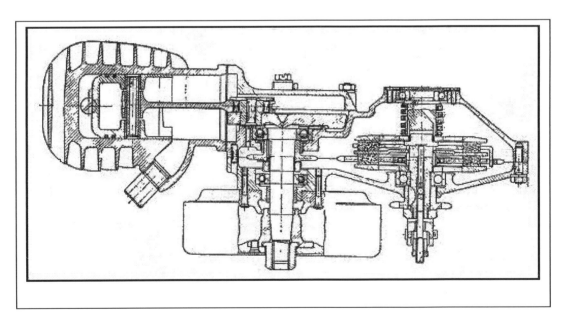

Cutaway of the famous Villiers Junior Engine. Versions of this engine powered the James, Rudge, Coventry-Eagle, Francis-Barnett, Dayton, Sun and New Hudson Autocycles.

Chapter Three

The European Autocycles and Cyclemotors

In the pioneering days of motor cycling in Europe the term "autocycle" meant any powered two-wheeler and was, therefore, synonymous with motor cycle. Even today, the governing body of motor cycle sport in England is the Auto Cycle Union. The reception of powered bicycles and light weight motorcycles was markedly different in the European countries than it was in the United States. For starters, the greater distances between cities and towns in the U.S. called for a more powerful machine or even a motor car.

In Europe, however, the compact nature (as compared with the United States) of the countryside lent a greater utility to smaller, less powerful vehicles, including two wheelers. In addition, the economic stresses caused by two world wars in the European theatre forced the adoption of less expensive transportation choices. Accordingly, a utilitarian style of motorcycle with pedals and a small engine, of between 75cc and 100cc capacity gained public and legal acceptance. In England the motorized bicycle continued to remain a popular means of transportation, due in part because of the tax advantages.

In 1931 the British government drastically lowered the annual tax rate of motor vehicles with engines of less than 150cc. This cheap rate insured the sales of small light motorcycles and motorized bicycles. Machines of this size were popular in the mainland of Europe and the aim of the British government was to help popularize this economical method of transport. It worked, for manufacturers offered many models throughout the period between the World Wars.

A large part of the story of powered bicycles in England is connected with the world famous engine manufacturer, Villiers. Even before the turn of the century, John Marsden was building bicycles in Wolverhampton, England called the "Sunbeam". Wishing to take advantage of the latest machinery, he purchased the most precise machines of the day from the American firm of Pratt & Whitney. When the equipment arrived, it was too large to fit within his building, so he built a new plant nearby which was located on Villiers Street and named the new operation the Villiers Cycle Components Company.

By 1912 they added a 2-stroke motorcycle engine to their product mix. The engine went through several variations, each improving the reliability and ease of starting. The world wide depression of the 1930s caused Villiers to develop a small, less expensive engine to appeal to manufacturers of motorized bicycles and autocycles, since the engines would qualify for the lower road taxes in most European countries. Villiers' long reputation for working with their customers led many bicycle companies to consider the addition of a Villiers engine.

This is the prototype of the small Villiers engine that was to power so many bicycles.

One of the first to take advantage of this lower rate was the Cyc-Auto. This design placed a 98cc. engine low just in front of the bottom bracket of a regular diamond-frame bicycle, driving the rear wheel by means of a chain on the left side. The vehicle was marginally heavier than a regular bicycle and could be pedaled in the same manner, so it appealed to those who did not wish the power of a larger motorcycle. This type of motorized bicycle became generally known in Britain as an autocycle.

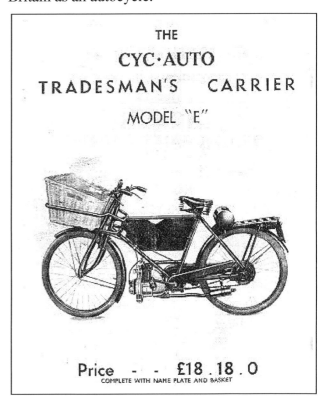

The Cyc-Auto was a popular delivery vehicle.

Raynal was among the first companies to use the 98 cc Villiers "Junior" engine that would be adopted to power autocycles and mopeds from other manufacturers. It was reported that the Villiers Junior was designed specifically for the Raynal but Villiers, apprehensive that the Raynal would not achieve a high volume of sales, 'leaked' the design details to Excelsior to ensure a larger market for their new engine. The Excelsior design looked very similar to the Raynal, placing the Villiers engine down low to produce a fine riding machine that rode very similar to a regular bicycle.

The Excelsior (British) used the Villiers Junior engine on their motorized bicycle.

Excelsior was one of several trademarks used by the old established company of Bayliss, Thomas & Company. Founded in 1874, the company had a long history of making bicycles and tricycles at the Excelsior Works in Lower Ford Street, Coventry. The Bayliss, Thomas name was still used for some exports since there were other companies in Germany and the USA which had rights to the Excelsior name.

Following the introduction of these two machines, production of autocycles blossomed with James, Rudge, Coventry-Eagle, Francis-Barnett, Norman, Three Spires, Dayton, Sun and New Hudson all producing similar, Junior-powered autocycles. The James Cycle Company Ltd of Greet, Birmingham was founded in 1880 by Harry James and was, therefore, a well-established manufacturer of both pedal cycles and motor cycles when it introduced its model J18 autocycle for the 1938 season. The early version had a small fuel tank, no springing and no engine covers; inverted levers were used for the brakes. Like all of James's machines at the time, a Villiers engine powered it. Although the company went into the wartime production of armaments and aircraft parts, it continued to produce some autocycles for civilian use.

Rudge-Whitworth Limited was founded in Coventry in 1894 by the merger of two bicycle manufacturers; the Rudge Cycle Company and the Whitworth Cycle company. Rudge-Whitworth produced many very high quality bicycles and motor cycles but, the world wide depression hit the company and left it almost destitute. The company decided to try to manufacture one last product, and as the world geared up for war, autocycles were one of the ways of transportation still being allowed to be manufactured. So Rudge also used the Villiers "Junior" engine to power an autocycle.

New Hudson

New Hudson was a British manufacturer of motorcycles from 1903 until the early 1930s, when the company changed to the manufacture of Girling brakes. New Hudson also produced a wide range of regular bicycles. Early in 1940 they returned to powered two wheelers with an autocycle, but the New Hudson autocycle is chiefly remembered as a post-war machine. This is probably because the later models were the most popular of all the British autocycles and New Hudson continued autocycle production much later than any of its competitors did.

The autocycle was launched in March 1940 and was powered by the Villiers JDL engine. It was unsprung and had no engine covers but was otherwise typical of a JDL-powered autocycle. When production recommenced after the war New Hudson had become part of the cycle division of BSA. For 1948, the machine was fitted with pressed steel blade girder forks, plus engine shields and other detail improvements. New Hudson attempted to update the old design, giving it an appearance more akin to the mopeds that were rapidly taking over from the autocycles. At this time, most of the other makes of autocycle were disappearing from the market in the face of the moped onslaught. The New Hudson continued to be sold until 1958, but that year saw the end of the Villiers 2F engine, so the New Hudson also left the market.

The Anzani Bicycle Engine

Alessandro Ambrogio Anzani was born in Italy in 1877 but moved to France as a young man to race and build motorcycles. He designed and built his own motorcycle. From his race winnings, he set up a small workshop near Paris in 1907. The French aviator Louis Blériot adapted Anzani's motorcycle engine to his aeroplane and used this engine to make the first flight across the English Channel. This brought Anzani fame and allowed him to build and develop multi-cylinder aircraft engines that grew so popular that Anzani was able to build factories both in Britain and in Italy.

In 1921, Anzani's continuing experiments led to thoughts of motorizing bicycles, resulting in the building of a compact, belt driven 4-stroke engine of 75cc capacity. These small engines were designed to be easily fitted to normal bicycles and economically running some 70 to 100 miles on a single gallon of fuel. Anzani produced the cyclemotor as a kit to motorize a bicycle and it was shown at the 1922 Paris Salon. The intended market was not the general public but cyclemakers that were looking for a small engine to add to their bicycles. Arguably, the Anzani clip-on engine may be among the earliest of pioneering lightweight clip-on cyclemotor engines destined to become so popular in the post WWII period.

The Anzani Cycle Motor of 1922

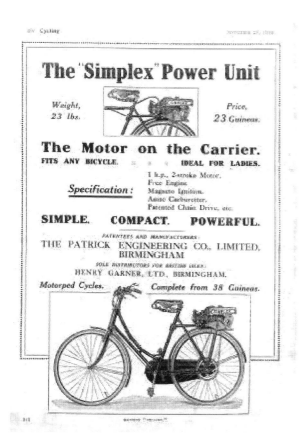

The British Simplex was a different company from the American Simplex.

Ettore Bugatti's Cyclemotor

Possibly the most complex cyclemotor ever designed was created by Ettore Bugatti during World War II for cheap transportation after the war. During the war Bugatti was barred from his factory at Moisheim so he camped out in Paris. There he worked on multiple projects to be undertaken after the war ended. His Type 72 Cyclemotor engine was a double overhead cam 10.6 cc single cylinder air-cooled engine that incorporated a Roots-type supercharger. The crankcase and head were to be made of aluminum with a finned steel cylinder and a roller-bearing connecting rod. Peak power was expected to be produced at 15,000 rpm.

Although the engine never went into production, some parts were made and at least two mostly complete engines have been located. A second version of the engine indicates that development work continued after the war. Ettore Bugatti died in 1947 only months after his factory in Moisheim was legally returned to him.

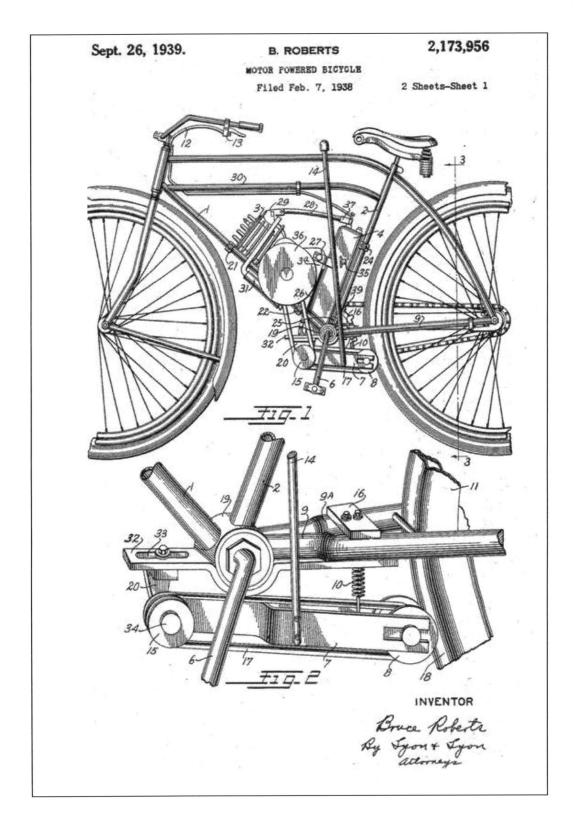

As the patent of the original 1938 Whizzer shows, the engine transmitted torque to the rear wheel by means of a friction roller. The friction drive was changed to a belt drive in 1941.

Chapter Four

The Whizzer Story

Ride One and You'll Buy One

Up until this past decade, the most successful embodiment of a true motorized bicycle that has been produced in the United States has been arguably the Whizzer. I am defining a "true" motorized bike as one that can still function as a normal bicycle but one that can also be ridden as a motorbike. The problems of designing an add-on motor attachment to a bicycle are many, starting with the problem of engine placement. The most advantageous area for balance purposes is to place engine within the frame tube triangle, that is, down between the rider's legs, like a motorcycle. The problem with this placement is that virtually all available small air-cooled engines are simply too wide. The standard bicycle pedal arms are only about 5" to 5-1/2" wide, so either the engine must be placed much higher in the frame triangle, or the pedal arms must be drastically shortened or widened past what is practical to propel the bicycle. And if the engine is raised (which also raises the center of gravity that must be balanced), there still remains the problem of lining up the drive train. That is, the power take-off sprocket of the engine will sit three to four inches to the right (or left) of the rear wheel, necessitating a jack shaft and additional sprockets and still another chain (with the original pedal chain still on the left, this brings the total up to three separate chains) to line up with the rear wheel.

Then there is the problem of providing for a clutch system to disconnect the power when stopping or waiting for a traffic signal. Earlier designs simply did not provide for a clutch, so the rider was forced to kill the engine and re-start it at every stop. And still the problem of how the engine is to be started remains. Pull start, pedal start, push start, or kick start? Overcoming these sorts of design problems probably deterred the majority of do-it-your builders who considered tackling the motorizing of a bicycle.

Enter the Whizzer. This one took a different perspective toward the design problems of motorizing a standard bicycle. Instead of using a production engine, the designer, Bruce Roberts of Hollywood, CA, started with a blank sheet and created a slim-line engine especially adapted to fit into the narrow triangle of a production bicycle. Roberts was well aware of the problems of engine placement:

> *"...Another object of my invention is to provide a motor structure of sufficient power and efficiency yet sufficiently narrow and limited in size as to be attached to a conventional bicycle within the limits of the central frame structure and between the planes in which the pedal cranks revolve."* From the 1938 patent application of Bruce Roberts.

Roberts was awarded a patent for his invention in 1939 and assigned the patent rights to Breene-Taylor Engineering of Los Angeles, CA. Breen-Taylor's main business was in manufacturing parts for the aircraft industry, so they had experience in making light aluminum parts. Their facilities were ideal for producing the gas tank, the aluminum crankcase, and the precision parts necessary for a light-weight 4-cycle air-cooled engine.

By specifying an extremely narrow design, Roberts had solved the engine placement problem. The first iteration transmitted the power to the rear wheel by means of a friction roller; this not only eliminated an extra chain, but also provided for a clutching action by rotating the drive roller away from the rear tire. Mainly though, the completed kits simply looked great. The central placement of the engine and the motorcycle-styled tank captured the look that boys were seeking and the finished result fairly screamed "light-weight motorcycle!" The first kits sold for $54.95, produced about 1.375 horsepower and included the 2/3 gallon fuel tank. The carburetor, which was made in-house by Breene-Taylor, was mounted to a swivel-jointed intake manifold which allowed the carb float to sit level on different bicycle frames.

"WHIZZER" Bicycle Motor. Quiet, Dependable, 4-cycle, 1⅜ h.p. Bicycle structure not weakened. Center of gravity unchanged. Looks like motorcycle. Easily installed. Further information write:
BREENE-TAYLOR ENGINEERING CORP.
7016 McKinley   **Los Angeles.**

The engine and drive train clamped onto the bike frame with a three-point mount, which stayed basically the same throughout all the models. The early drive system was by rollers driven by a V-belt. The belt forced the bottom rear roller against the rear tires. There was no

CHAPTER 4

clutch or transmission but the drive could be tensioned via a cable that mounted to the tank. Known as the Model "D", approximately 1,000 of these first units were sold in late 1939 and early 1940.

From the lessons learned in the first year of production, Breene-Taylor changed the cylinder head to aluminum for better cooling, tweaked the camshaft for more power, and added an oil dipstick to check the oil level. Another patent was filed on the improvements in the compression release and internal oil pump. This newer version was known as the Model "E" Whizzer. As with any completely new engine design, problems such as crankshaft reliability and leaks from the two-piece split crankcase caused the factory to have to replace some engines with improved versions. By 1942, with the war effort into full production, approximately 1500 Model "E" bicycle motors had been produced.

Meanwhile Breene-Taylor was deluged with aircraft-type orders from the ramped-up war production efforts. Sales from the bicycle engine manufacturing operation was not as profitable as war contracts, so they sold the patent rights and all molds and tooling for the Whizzer to one of the original investors, Dietrich Kohlsatt, and Martin Goldman, one of the attorneys for Breene-Taylor.

Kohlsatt and Goldman wished to continue the engine business so they set up and began a new company known as the Whizzer Motor Company. In a move that was to pay huge dividends in the future, they convinced Henry Schuricht, who had been an engineer for Breene-Taylor, to come with the new Whizzer Motor Company. He was the person responsible for the designs of the later engines, "H", "J", "300" and "700". The new company began by subcontracting almost all of the parts production to nearby machine shops and foundries. But subcontracting parts also brought problems in quality control and meeting delivery times. There were indications that some of Whizzer's customer complaints came from sub-standard parts purchased from the outside contractors.

By this time the U.S. was on wartime economy and all manufacturing output was beginning to be strictly controlled by the War Production Board (WPB). The War Production Board was established as a government agency on January 16, 1942 by executive order of President Franklin D. Roosevelt. The purpose of the board was to regulate the production and allocation of materials and fuel during World War II in the United States. The WPB converted and expanded peacetime industries to meet war needs, allocated scarce materials vital to war production, established priorities in the distribution of materials and services, and prohibited nonessential production. It rationed such things as gasoline, heating oil, metals, rubber, and plastics.

During this time, any company had to get permission from the WPB to manufacture any item that was not covered under an existing government contract. Somehow, Goldman was able to convince the WPB that producing bicycle engines would allow workers to be able to commute to wartime jobs and save gasoline at the

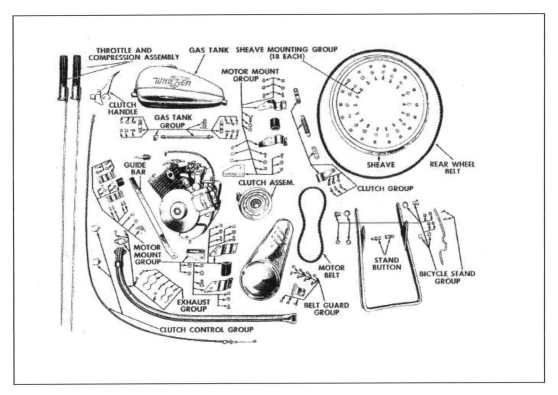

When a Whizzer customer purchased a kit, everything to motorize a bicycle was sent, including wiring, nuts and bolts, drive belt, all throttle controls, and a complete manual.

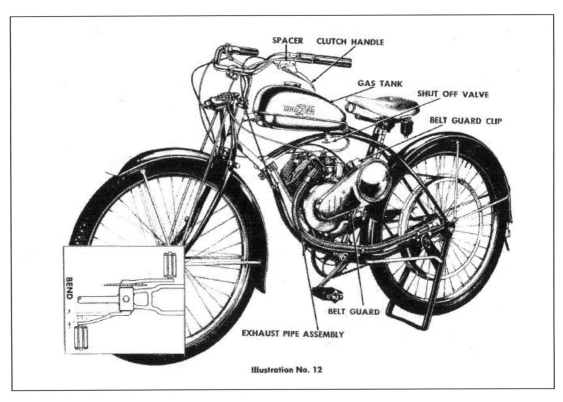

When properly assembled, this is what the customer should have. Note the instructions for bending (if necessary) the pedal arms. Most did not need to be bent.

same time. The Whizzer Motor Company was granted the permission to produce this gas-saving method of getting the defense plants workers to their jobs, but Whizzer was to restrict the sales of their new model engines for "defense workers only". Henry Schuricht used this opportunity to make several improvements in the drive train. Schuricht dropped the friction drive system and adopted a belt-drive system that used a v-belt to transmit the power to the rear wheel. To accomplish this, he developed a belt sheave that bolted to the spokes of the rear wheel. Whizzer also changed to a new five quart gas tank that remained in production of the life of the unit.

With the ending of the war in 1945 there arose a huge demand for powered vehicles of any kind. All types of consumer goods were in great demand as the nation shifted from a wartime economy to a booming civilian economy. Virtually no automobiles or motorcycles (other than those for the military) had been produced during the war, so the Whizzer Motor Company was in the right place at the right time with a vastly improved product. In 1945 Whizzer was able to offer their new model, which as introduced as the "Model F" to the general public that was clambering for any type of motorized transportation.

Since Whizzer had been contracting out almost all of its foundry work, the company made the decision to move from southern California to Pontiac, Michigan, a center of foundries and automobile-parts subcontractors. The Pontiac area had experienced explosive growth in manufacturing facilities during the wartime and now that the boom had ended, the companies located there were eagerly seeking new customers. The larger foundries were offering to serve smaller companies whom they had turned away during the war. Schuricht especially wished to work with the Wilson Foundry & Machine in Pontiac. The Wilson Foundry had developed an outstanding reputation for the precision casting of automobile engine blocks. In Pontiac Whizzer would contract out a large portion of the engine parts.

By 1946 Schuricht had almost completely redesigned the crankcase from a split two-piece to a complex deep casting with a side cover. This stopped the oil leaks for good. He also improved the bearings to give a longer life and improved the valve tappets. He switched to a Tillotson carburetor to replace the older Breene-Taylor carb. The new model, introduced in the summer of 1946, was known as the Model "H" which became known for its reliability and therefore was the best seller of all the engine series, with sales of approximately 139,000 units.

With the increase in sales came the recognition from bicycle manufacturers that opportunities existed in producing a bicycle expressly designed for the addition of a motor. One of the first to jump on the motorized bicycle bandwagon was the established bicycle manufacturer, Cleveland Welding, manufacturer of the Roadmaster bicycle. In 1947 the company produced a version of the Roadmaster specifically tailored for the addition of a Whizzer motor. The bicycle came with wider wheel rims, heavier-duty spokes, a headlight, a spring front fork, and a New Departure front hub brake. The frame was altered slightly on the left rear side to add clearance for the drive belt. It made a perfect chassis for the Whizzer unit and when completed actually became a good handling light motorbike.

However, not long after production was initiated, the cantilever style frame used by Cleveland Welding was seen by some (read lawyers) as too close a copy of a Schwinn frame, which was the subject of a design patent. In order not to cause difficulties with this industry giant, Whizzer pulled production from Cleveland Welding and

gave it to Schwinn. To produce a frame for the Whizzer motor, Schwinn took their heavy duty frame and made a few minor changes. They notched the rear fender and frame for belt clearance, added thicker spokes, and heavier coils in the spring fork and installed a front drum brake. These were sold as complete bikes through Schwinn dealers and were designated "WZ" models. The first Schwinn WZ came out in 1947. Schwinn also modified a Schwinn Cycle truck delivery bike into the "Powercycle Truck" bikes

In 1948 Whizzer announced the Model "J" engine, which came with a chrome-plated exhaust and motorcycle-type twist-grip controls. They also switched to a more reliable Carter carburetor. Sales of the Model J topped 50,000 units. Although the company continued producing and selling engine kits, the success of the completely finished motorized bicycle caused them to think again about producing a complete unit with the motor already installed on a bicycle especially built for them. The sales dollar volume per unit soared with the complete bike and engine.

So in the summer of 1948 Whizzer announced the availability of the Whizzer Pacemaker, built on 24" heavy duty wheels with a telescoping front fork and a Sturmey-Archer front drum brake and a regular rear coaster brake produced by New Departure. The engine for the Pacemaker was engineered by Whizzer's Henry Schuricht and Vince Piggins of Wilson Foundry--the same Vince Piggins who was later behind the Hudson Hornet's NASCAR championships in the 1950s and who developed what became Chevrolet's Z/28 package in 1967. With the new engine design, the Pacemaker achieved a top speed of 40 mph. After an initial 500 or so were produced by Whizzer, the rest of the bikes were produced by Schwinn. Slight variations of this version would continue to be sold through 1952.

For 1949 Whizzer began to have Schwinn weld some of the engine mount brackets to the frame, since this really speeded up the assembly process and created a stronger engine mount. A new option offered by the factory was a chrome-plated bolt-on generator to provide power for a lighting package. The color of virtually all Pacemakers was slightly different shades of maroon.

The 1950 models continued with just a few changes. A major change occurred in 1952 when Whizzer switched from a flywheel magneto to a generator. Since the generator was used for ignition and lighting purposes only (not for charging a battery), they all were actually alternators. Although the company ceased producing the Pacemaker after 1952, leftover unsold models were still being marketed by some dealers in 1953 and 1954.

In November of 1949 Whizzer also began producing a motorized bicycle that had 20" wheels instead of the usual 24". This model, called the "Sportsman", was radically different from the previous models. Because the 20" wheels caused the bicycle to be so low, Whizzer did away with the normal pedal assembly at the bottom (which would not have cleared the ground, anyway), and added a kick starter in the place of the regular pedal start. The first of these bikes were rumored to have been created by one of the plant employees for his son, and the finished result was so appealing that the company put it into production. Later, the company produced a 24" wheel version of this kick-start configuration called the "Ambassador".

The beginning of the import mini-bikes in the middle 1950s began to take its toll of the sales of the regular Whizzer. As the sales began to slow Whizzer began to look at producing other items. In 1955 the Whizzer Motor Company changed names to become Whizzer Industries and began to produce windows, sliding doors, as well as children's toys and wagons. The company continued to offer Whizzer engines and bicycles from the previously unsold stock until about 1964 when the factory closed its doors due to lack of demand. In 1970 a collector purchased all remaining stocks of

The Whizzer "Sportsman" featured a much lower look with 20" wheels, no pedals, and a kick starter.

This classic Whizzer is built on a straight bar frame with the Schwinn springer front fork. Note how precisely the engine must fit into the triangle opening.

This beautifully restored Whizzer is on display at Barber Motorsports Museum in Birmingham, AL.

parts and inventory of what was left of the Whizzer engine portion. The Whizzer remained a popular item among collectors of post-war motorbikes and parts were eagerly sought by restorers and enthusiasts. Whizzer clubs and newsletters continued to keep the memory alive and restored Whizzer prices began to climb. But the Whizzer had such appeal for motorized bicycle enthusiasts that it was inevitable that attempts would be made to bring it back to life.

The Whizzer is Reborn

By the late 1970s and early 1980s resurgence in Whizzer nostalgia began to emerge. Restored Whizzers began to climb in price and the motorized bicycle was always a center of interest at vintage bike meets. This increased visibility was bound to attract the attention of entrepreneurial types. In 1992 an attempt to bring back the Whizzer was made by a group in southern California. The idea seems to have been to create a sort of Whizzer replica using the internals of a modern engine with the external look of the older engine. Accordingly, an entirely new engine was designed around a Kohler K91 crank, rod, and piston fitted inside a new high silicon aluminum cylinder and crankcase, affording about the same engine capacity as the original. The gas tank resembled the classic Whizzer tank only it was made in fiberglass. The ignition was entirely electronic and a Mikuni carburetor was fitted. Unfortunately, much more development work was needed to thoroughly debug the new engine and the limited resources did not allow the company time to accomplish this. The result was a short-lived and not very successful endeavor. The Whizzer revival awaited much more capital and resources.

In 1997 a group of investors was able to purchase the Whizzer trademark and all manufacturing rights to the Whizzer engine and drive system. They located a manufacturer in Taiwan and began tooling up to make a close replica of the original engine and drive system. For starters, they were completely successful in maintaining the original "Whizzer" look that devotees loved so much. The gas tank was a perfect copy of the original. The frame was a close replica of the popular "cantilever" style that most original Whizzers used. The new management team made several important simplifying and economical updates to the engine. They kept the original concept of a thin-line crankcase and 4-cycle flathead engine. For durability and economy, they replaced the original points and magneto with a far more reliable (and cheaper) CDI (capacitive discharge ignition) electronic ignition tied to a 12 volt electrical system with battery. They adopted a newer design motorcycle-type carburetor with an improved choke system. For the Department of Transportation, they added multiple reflectors and bright turn signals. They included an improved drum-type both front and rear brake system, which offered a far safer motoring package.

Although their advertisements stated the engine output was 3 horsepower and the bike's top speed was 25 miles per hour, the words "approximately" gave a wink and an indication that the real output was more like 4 to 5 horsepower and the top speed was close to 40 miles per hour. Offered at first only in the color of Maroon, the bike was available with 24" or 26" wheels. Making the 12-gauge stainless steel spokes a standard item was a welcome addition and the chrome muffler, belt guard, and luggage rack polished off the package, along with a one year warranty.

Even the original purists were pleased. The new Whizzer had captured the "look" so well that the new models were not shunned but eagerly snapped up by many. True, at a selling price of $1850 (in 1998), the new Whizzers did not approach the 3-4 thousand dollar prices that original Whizzers were bringing, but still offered a remarkable value for a retro-styled product that brought back memories of the 40s and 50s. And the reliability of electronic ignition and additional safety features was a distinct plus.

In 1998 a new Classic model was offered in black and it too found favor with collectors and some motorcycle enthusiasts. One small black cloud appeared on the horizon concerning the Whizzer's cranking system. In all honesty, pedal-starting a 148cc. 4-stroke single cylinder engine at the same time while pedaling a 97 pound motorbike is not easy; many found it difficult if not daunting. Many first-time riders not used to manipulating the compression-release starting mechanism found cranking the motorbikes difficult.

So in March of 1998 Whizzer announced a new model, the Ambassador, built more along the lines of a light motorcycle. It came with an electric start and retro chopper styling; quite a difference from the original motorized bicycle look. In July 1998, Whizzer added a CVT (continuously variable transmission) to the Ambassador line, which apparently was so popular that Whizzer later offered a CVT option to their Classic model. For a short while in 2004-2005 the Whizzer Company toyed with the concept of selling the engine kits alone, but later dropped the idea and continued selling the complete package. Today the company sells complete retro-styled motorbikes, Whizzer accessories, and Whizzer collectibles both direct to customers and through Whizzer dealers.

The New Whizzer can be identified by the telescopic-type front fork, the multiple reflectors and the center stand. This one has front and rear disk brakes.

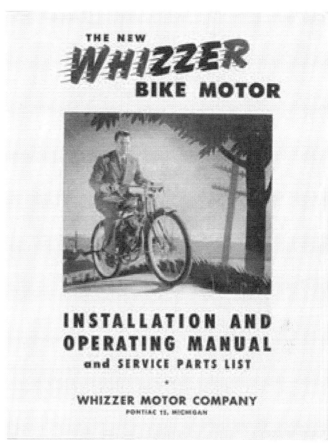

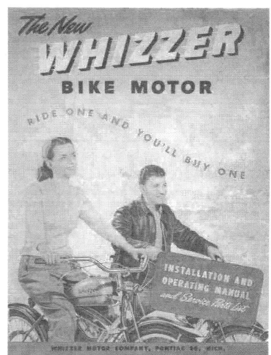

Front cover of the Whizzer Owners Manual.

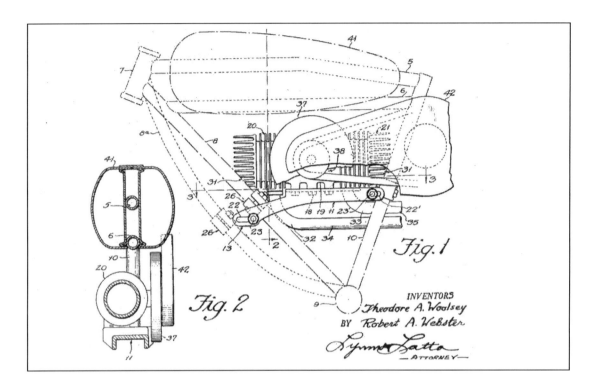

In this drawing from the patents of the Jac & Heintz twin cylinder bike engine, the engine is deftly fitted into the bicycle frame triangle. The cylinders are slightly offset to the left.

The DynaCycle engine actually replaced the regular bicycle pedals, effectively converting the bike into a light weight motorcycle. The elimination of pedals and the engine size of 165cc. required the DynaCycle to be registered as a motorcycle.

Chapter Five

The American Scene in the 50s and 60s

The Whizzer story is both a success story and a story of the decline of sales, but other entrepreneurs at about the same time tried to make a success of providing a kit for motorizing a bicycle. One that tried just after the end of World War II was unusual because of its twin cylinder nature. Twin cylinder bicycle motors were rare—the Johnson Brothers motor discussed earlier comes to mind—mainly because the bulk of two cylinders made them hard to fit into the bicycle frame. The Johnson Brothers motor fit on top of the rear wheel where the bike luggage rack normally fit. But a horizontally-opposed twin cylinder bicycle motor kit was offered just after the end of WW II by the Jack & Heintz Company.

Co-founders William S. Jack and Ralph M. Heintz formed Jack & Heintz, Ltd. in Palo Alto, California in 1940. In November of that year they moved their operations to Ohio and changed their company name slightly to Jack & Heintz, Inc. Mr. Jack was a successful manufacturing executive and Mr. Heintz was an electrical and mechanical engineer. Together, their company was a major contributor to the war effort, designing and manufacturing airplane starters, automatic pilots, motors, and other aircraft parts.

After the war ended the company searched for products to produce for the civilian market and one of the first was the twin cylinder bicycle engine kit. Reportedly, the engine was originally designed to be an aircraft drone engine, hence the two cylinders that had been adopted to drive a bicycle. The engine was used to power the Marman Twin, a motorized bike that Herbert "Zeppo" Marx produced in 1948 and 1949 at Marman Products Co. of Inglewood, CA. Zeppo Marx, who had teamed with brothers Harpo, Chico and Groucho until 1934, started the Marman Products Co. in 1941 to produce an improved type of heavy duty band clamp that became known as the "Marman Clamp." During World War II Zeppo's company produced the Marman Clamps used to hold the "Fat Man" atomic bomb inside the B-29 bomber, Bockscar. After the war Zeppo began to look for additional products to keep his factory busy.

The Marman Twin sported a chrome-plated gas tank and twin exhaust pipes.

Although sales of the Marman Twin were initially encouraging, by 1952 the post-war boom had died down, and the Marman Twin disappeared from the scene. Marman Products Co. was bought by Aeroquip which is still in business today.

However, Jack & Heintz continued to produce their twin cylinder engines for bicycle motors and produced the J & H Twin built on a Schwinn cantilever chassis with a springer front fork and a front drum brake. Like the Whizzer, the bike was belt driven by a sheave that bolted to the spokes of the rear wheel. The gas tank was slightly larger than the Whizzer but the looks were very similar.

A bicycle engine kit that completely replaced the crank and the pedals was introduced in 1948 was the DynaCycle. Using a 2-stroke engine of 165 cc, the designer, Frank Thomas, an engineer who had worked at Oak Ridge National Laboratories during World War II, brought to production a design that was extremely low mounted. The kit was designed to fit the standard 26" bicycle but recommended heavier gauge spokes on both wheels. Although the design worked, it really converted the bicycle into a light weight motorcycle, since the resulting machine could not be pedaled. Nor could the result combination still meet most legal definitions as a bicycle or moped. In addition, a regular bicycle is a poor chassis for a small motorcycle unless it is reinforced in many areas. As a last-ditch effort, the company introduced a complete motorbike with a reinforced frame. But sales were disappointingly small, so after undergoing reorganization, the company faded from sight in 1951.

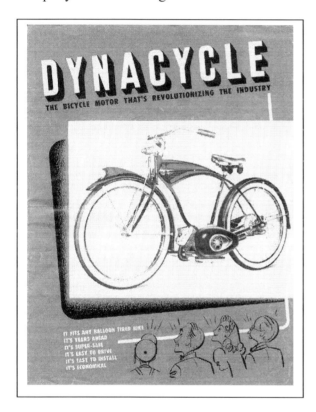

However, not all motorized bicycles disappeared after the demise of the Whizzer, although offerings from the United States were greatly diminished. A half-dozen or so manufacturers offered engines and engine kits during the 50s, 60s and 70s while magazines such as *Popular Mechanics* and *Mechanix Illustrated* still ran an occasional article on do-it-yourself motorizing of bicycles. The dream of a perfect motorized bicycle never died and inventors continued to apply for patents to introduce their idea of the perfect union.

One of the most successful teams of engine builders was the team of Irving Ohlsson and Harry Rice. Ohlsson, born in California in 1913, was a young devotee of model airplanes by the age of 18 had won 11 major model airplane contests with his rubber-band powered models. One was for a record-setting flight of 1 hour and 3 minutes reaching an altitude of 4300 feet and flying over 30 miles. Ohlsson then turned his attention to gasoline engines for model airplanes. In 1932 he adapted a 30 cc. gas engine designed for model boats to a 8-foot model airplane of his own design. Entered in a contest in Sacramento, Ohlsson's plane stayed aloft for 1 hour and 6 minutes, setting a record that would remain for several years. The plane was spotted by a private pilot at an altitude of 5,500 feet.

After graduating from high school Ohlsson went to work for Douglas Aircraft but he really wanted to open his own model shop in Los Angeles. Ohlsson had a few ideas about the construction of model airplane engines he wished to pursue. With the help of his friend Harry Rice, a machinist, Ohlsson began to manufacture his own line of engines and later added model airplane kits that he had designed and manufactured.

In 1941 Ohlsson and Rice started their own model airplane engine manufacturing business, producing engines that gained a solid reputation for reliability, ease of starting, and long life. World War II, however, soon put a temporary hold on their manufacturing business as all non-critical manufacturing was curtailed. As soon as the war was over, Ohlsson and Rice began operating around the clock producing engines. By 1947 their daily output was almost a thousand engines a day. They also began to manufacture glow plugs, propellers, and model racecars.

The frantic pace of running a successful manufacturing company and the constant pressure to bring out new products brought the partnership of Ohlsson and Rice to an end in 1953, but not before they had produced well over half a million model airplane engines. Ohlsson went on to develop a line of glow plug fuel and also helped design and manufacture special igniters for the aerospace industry.

But Harry Rice was not finished with the engine business. Rice saw an opportunity in the gap between the smaller model airplane engines that ran on glow plugs and the larger 4 cycle lawnmower engines that ran on automotive gas. Rice believed the engines would need to run on automotive type gas, not specially-blended model airplane fuel and thus would need a reliable magneto to produce an adequate spark. Rice also developed a diaphragm-type carburetor that would work in any position. Over the next three years Rice designed a series of 2-cycle engines with 1.26 Cubic inch displacement that were rated at about ¾ horsepower. In the 1960s Rice began to produce the engines alone and then adapted the engine to provide power for a small chainsaw, a small generator, and finally a small add-on bicycle motor. The O & R bicycle motor fit over the front wheel and transferred the power by means of a friction roller, much similar to the Solex. The bright yellow color that Rice used for his bicycle engine caused someone to refer to it as "chicken-power."

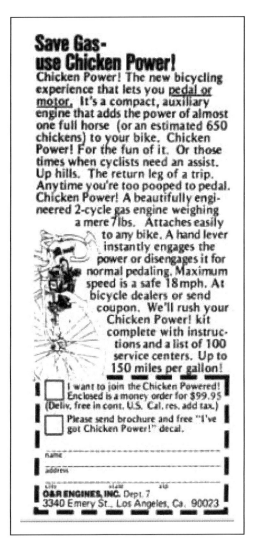

Rice thought the name was memorable so he began to advertise the O & R bicycle engine as the O & R "Chicken Power" engine. He advertised in national magazines and sold bicycle engine kits complete with gas tank, engine cover, and a friction roller that sat over the front tire and drove the front wheel. The engine proved to be reliable and started easily, but after a few years production it faded from the scene. Examples still show up periodically on eBay.

All the O&R bicycle motors proudly displayed the "Chicken Power" logo on the engine.

The Tanaka Bicycle motor sold by Sears drove the front wheel by means of a friction roller.

Another manufacturer of bicycle motors during the 70s and 80s was Tanaka Engines of Japan. Founded in 1917, the company produced recreational equipment long before they began manufacturing engines, but in the 1940s developed the "BK-3 Featherweight" bicycle engine. This was the predecessor of the engines later introduced into the United States.

Tanaka had a long history of manufacturing engines and motor parts. Their specialty was the casting and manufacture of industrial engine components. The first Tanaka engines to arrive on the North American continent were small outboard engines that were imported by Sears of Canada. In 1975 this was expanded to include a small bicycle engine that drove the front wheel by means of a hard rubber friction roller in much the same manner as the Solex and the O & R engines. The little engine was marketed by Sears & Roebuck in the United States as the "Free Spirit" bicycle assist motor

In the late 1970s Tanaka also supplied boat motors, small generators, pumps, and the above mentioned bicycle motors to Aquabug International, a small distributor out of New York State. The bicycle motors from Aquabug were sold under the "Bike-Bug" name and the "Aqua-Bug" name. All of the bicycle motors were 2-stroke engines of 23cc. In the early 80s the distributer suffered a financial setback, so it was purchased by the Tanaka Corporation. Tanaka dropped the other names and continued to market bicycle engines under the name "TAS Spitz". TAS was the name that Tanaka had been using for years for its line of small engines and small motorcycles.

When asked later about the reasons for dropping the bicycle motor kit in the later 1980s, a company official stated, "The market completely fell out. Nobody was buying them. Our motor kits sold for around $250.00 at that time. Honda was selling a complete 50cc bike package for around $400.00-$450.00. For less than twice the amount of a TAS Spitz, a complete vehicle with more power and higher top speed could be had. We just couldn't compete."

"300 mpg" is probably a little optimistic. "Auto-start" is not explained. The engine was started by pedaling the bicycle. I guest one could call that "auto-start".

The Buzz-Bee used a 2-cycle Power Products engine which was normally used to power lawn mowers. Being 2-stroke, it could run in any position, including this friction drive system.

CHAPTER 5

This is the Tanaka Bike Bug engine with the plastic cover removed. This engine was virtually identical to the Sears Free Spirit and the TAS Spitz.

The Saginaw Products Corp. of Saginaw, MI offered a kit that replaced the entire rear wheel with a motorized scooter wheel. It looked a little strange in the ads and stranger in person.

MOTORIZED BICYCLES

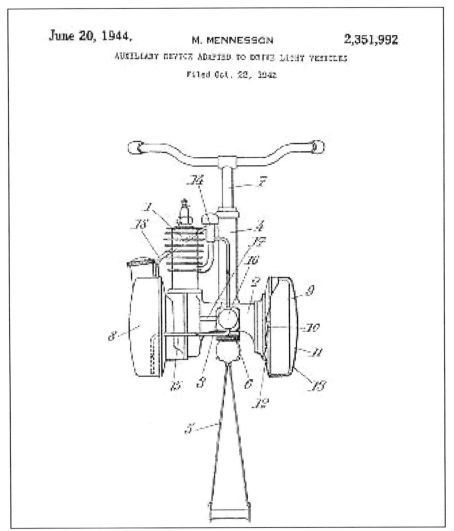

This U.S. patent was issued during World War II following a French patent in 1941. This bicycle motor later known as the Velosolex would prove to be the primary means of transportation for a war-torn France and most of Europe in the days just following the end of the war.

The Velosolex was sold either as a stand-alone engine or a complete bicycle with engine installed. This combination was the most popular one.

Chapter Six

Millions of Mopeds

The next chapter in the history of the motorized bicycle starts in Europe during the dark days of World War II, where the entire transportation system was being virtually destroyed. Fuel was increasingly hard to obtain and when available was poor in quality and scarce. In France, a company named "Solex," which was founded in 1905 by engineers Maurice Goudard and Marcel Mennesson, looked at the bleak transportation choices and made the bold move to do something about it. In 1941, Marcel Mennesson applied for a patent for a tiny gasoline engine that would sit atop the front wheel of a bicycle. A French Patent No. 462,902 was issued on 4 November 1941 while a US Patent No: 2,351,992 was issued on 22 October 1942.

With a capacity of just 38 cc and with a friction roller transmitting power to the wheel, the engine would provide just enough power to carry a normal sized rider without pedaling. The first prototype was completed in 1941 and installed on a bicycle. It had no clutch, but instead had to be stopped each time the bicycle came to a halt, but it cranked easily and proved a reliable source of power. The first 700 models were distributed to the employees of the company to aid in testing. A key improvement came from this extended testing with the development of a long-lasting roller made of carborundum, a super hard compound of silicon and carbon that was normally used for long wearing abrasives.

During the rest of the war the little engine continued to undergo testing and improvement. As the war ended, a vast need for motorized transportation began to emerge. No one could afford automobiles, much less a motorcycle. Most factories in Europe had been destroyed by the war. Since the bicycle had been an important part of the transportation system before the war, countries like France and Italy were quick to re-start production of bicycles. By 1946 the Solex Company was able to ramp up production of bicycles and motors which it marketed under the name Velosolex.

The Velosolex was mounted over the front wheel.

France's largest manufacturer of motorcycles, Motobecane, also jumped into the production of motorized bicycles after the war. Founded in 1922 by Charles Benoit and Abel Bardin, the company was also a major producer of bicycles. The word "Motobecane" was a combination of two slang words: "moto" was slang for motorcycle and "becane" was a slang term for bicycle. During the immediate post-war years the company diversified into manufacturing a motorized bicycle. Motobecane introduced a complete powered bicycle called the Mobylette in 1949. Over the next 48 years, Motobecane manufactured 14 million Mobylettes. In India the same model was manufactured under license by Mopeds India, Ltd. under the name Suvega.

The French bicycle and motorcycle manufacturer Peugeot had marketed a 50cc. motorized bicycle since 1932 that was moderately successful. However, the popularity of the Motobecane Mobylette spurred Peugeot to bring out their version called the PHV25 in 1949. Peugeot followed this with the Bima, which competed directly with the Mobylette. Like the Mobylette, the Bima was hugely popular and was followed by the BB2.

The Peugeot Bima

CHAPTER 6

Meanwhile in Italy during World War II, a Turin lawyer named Aldo Farinelli and an engineer named Aldo Leoni developed a small engine to power bicycles. They saw the potential market for inexpensive transportation after the war ended. In 1944, just after the country was liberated and before the end of the war, they announced their "Cucciolo", or "little puppy." By 1945 the demand for the engine was so great that the team contracted with the motorcycle manufacturer Ducati to produce the engines. In 1952, with 200,000 Cucciolos already sold, Ducati finally offered its own complete moped.

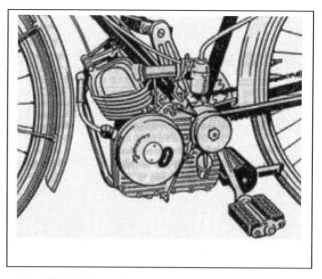

The "Little Puppy" was squeezed in just behind the front wheel. Notice how close the spark plug is to the front fender.

The Cucciolo was mounted just in front of the pedals.

Apart from the economy, part of the appeal of the motorized bicycle was the absence of legal restrictions; as long as the engine was less than 50cc (the original Velosolex was 33cc. but soon grew to 49cc.), students and others could ride a motorized bicycle with no driver's license or registration required. The Solex Company continued to produce the engine alone to be attached to a bicycle, but found that greater sales volume came from the production of both the bicycle and the engine attached. This combination proved to be the best selling mode of transportation in Europe. By 1948 the company had produced in excess of 25,000 units. The Velosolex Company has since sold more than 8 million powered bicycles worldwide, but mainly in Europe and Scandinavia. The powered 2-stroke became so popular in Europe that the oil company British Petroleum marketed a pre-mixed blend of gas and oil known as "Solexine". The fuel was sold in 2-liter cans.

Pre-blended 2-cycle oil and gasoline was sold by the 2-liter can.

The Term "Moped" is Invented

The term "moped" was coined by Swedish journalist Harald Nielsen in 1952 to describe a new motorized bike with a pressed steel frame from Steyr-Puch of Austria, a company founded by Johann Puch, a master bicycle maker in the late 1800s. The Puch moped was a radical departure from the motorized bicycles of the past. Although it still continued the use of pedal drive, the new moped featured fan-boosted engine cooling, a 2-speed transmission with handlebar shifting, and an electrical system that could drive a bright headlamp and adequate rear and turn signals. It also substituted a stamped steel frame for the prior bicycle tubing. This allowed for more strength and a way to pass the electrical wires and handlebar controls through the middle of the frame.

Known as the Puch MS-50, it became so successful that the basic features were copied by most moped manufacturers worldwide. In the late 1950s the Puch was marketed in the United States by Sears as the Allstate Mo-Ped.

Puch Maxi

As Europe began to recover from the devastation of the war, most industry executives predicted that the mopeds would be replaced by motorcycles and automobiles, but in Europe the moped continued to sell. It was adopted by the younger set, movie stars, and models. True, virtually no one ever pedaled the moped, for it was cumbersome and heavy compared to a bicycle. But it was approachable and easy to ride; students and beginners did not feel intimidated. More importantly, it was legal. Mopeds became a socially accepted way of traveling, at least in Europe. They are used for commuting to and from work and school. There, mopeds are often used as light delivery vehicles. This is especially true in Italy, where the popular Vespa Ciao Porter is an everyday workhorse.

Although the Vespa Ciao Porter is rated for 250 lbs., it is regularly seen carrying 500 lbs.

The French exported their Solexes and Motobecanes to their former colonies in Southeast Asia, where they found instant acceptance. The Dutch shipped mopeds to Indonesia where the bikes were quickly adopted for their cheap, efficient transportation.

The Sears Mo-Ped was actually a Puch moped with the Sears name on the tank. It was a well-proven design that offered good value for the price.

The advertising copy says it best. Honda single-handedly changed the cycling world with its quality, commitment to excellence, and products.

Gas or Electric powered bikes...Two or three wheels!

Prices starting at $699.00

Gas Engine Specifications
- 25 cc. gas engine
- Front and rear brake
- Friction roller drive
- 120-160 mpg
- 20 miles per hour
- Springer front fork
- Various models available

Made in the U.S.A.

Electric Trike
- 24 volt brushless motor
- 8 to 10 miles per hour
- Up to 10 mile range
- Parking brake
- 5-speed pedal drive

Electric Cruiser
- 24 v. brushless
- Up tp 15 mph
- 15 mile range
- Blue/Silver 2 tone
- 5 speed pedal drive

Call toll free 1-877-947-2453
ZIPCYCLE
20 Adkins Road
Double Springs, AL 35553
See us on the web at www.zipcycle.com
Or email us at micropower@sonet.net

THE BIKE YOU WANTED AS A KID
AND NOW YOU CAN AFFORD.........

The Zipcycle was built on a classic cantilever frame.

Chapter Seven

The Zen of the Zipcycle

During the 1980s and 1990s, I was one of two partners in a small fabrication shop where, after regular hours in our full-time careers, we spent most evenings and weekends producing CNC wood carving machines and restoring vintage sports cars to have fun. It was a great place to hang out and there was always some project that we were working on. Our CNC machines paid the bills and allowed us to assemble a fairly well-equipped general metal fabrication facility with most basic machine tools including lathes, milling machines and welding equipment for both aluminum and steel. My partner, Gary Rogers, was a gifted engineer who could literally build anything that he set his mind to, from hang gliders to ultralight airplanes to robotic machines. When Gary was finally able to retire from his full time position, I asked him what he planned to do with some of his newly-earned free time. He replied that he had always wanted to perfect an engine driven bicycle, one that was truly dual-purpose (that is, one that could still be used as a pedal bicycle but with auxiliary engine power). In addition, he did not want to place the engine above the front or rear wheel (for this upset the normal balance of a bike), but down in the normal motorcycle engine position. We had long admired the look of the old Whizzers and had both owned and ridden motorbikes and motorscooters when we were teenagers. I considered this to be a perfect project for a couple of old gear-heads, so I enthusiastically signed on.

I recalled that my Homelite string trimmer had a very compact engine arrangement, so I suggested that I would donate it to his experiments. My calculations had indicated that the 25 cc. engine (developing about 1.1 HP) should be sufficient to propel a rider to about 20-25 miles per hour, or about as fast as one should travel safely on a regular bicycle. We went to Wal-Mart, purchased a cruiser bicycle, and Gary started. In order to not alter the normal pedal drive arrangement, Gary designed a friction-roller drive system that did not interfere with the original chain drive, leaving it completely intact and unchanged. Shades of the original Whizzer!

This is what we started with—the business end of a Homelite String trimmer. A very compact 1.1 horse power 2-stroke engine.

By the following weekend, he had a working motorbike. We tried it out and were delighted by the results. Gary's design rode and balanced exactly like a regular bicycle, was easy to start with the pedal-starting system he had designed, and had sufficient power to carry a normal-sized rider on virtually any terrain. For the more challenging hills, the rider could add his own leg power to assist. The drive roller was spring-loaded into the rear tire, and although it worked reasonably well, required a very strong grip to release with the hand clutch. So I asked Gary if he could come up with an easier-to-operate clutch mechanism. After several variations, he developed an over-center cam-type clutch that was easy to release and required no springs, but gave an excellent transfer of power. It cantilevered the weight of the engine to press the drive roller into the tire.

To optimize the drive roller, we made extensive tests of every type of roller from knurled aluminum (too abrasive on the rear tire) to skateboard wheels. We had the greatest success with modified skateboard wheels, so we sent a skateboard wheel off to a chemical lab and found it was primarily polyurethane. A little research disclosed that polyurethane could be compounded to any Shore hardness (an industry measure of firmness) from rock-hard to gummy soft. We tested the Shore hardness of a street tire and ordered polyurethane rollers that were just slightly harder than the tire compound (this was so that the majority of wear would be on the tire). The result was a drive roller that gave an excellent grip, but was long wearing. We found we could ride in the rain or morning dew without slipping. The choice of a suitable drive roller really enhanced the friction-drive package.

Seen with the cover removed, the engine drove a toothed belt to a Nylon gear (to provide the proper gear ratio) to a polyurethane friction roller

Gary named the result "The Zipcycle", and we began to produce a few prototypes. We ran the prototypes daily and if something broke we reinforced the part to make it stronger. We tried variations of final gearing to arrive at an optimum ratio. A taller gear gave a higher top speed, but not enough low speed pulling torque. The final gear ratio selected produced about 22-25 miles per hour on a level surface with a moderate hill-climbing ability. We eventually advertised a top speed of 20 mph so no one would complain. Since we had used a single speed rear coaster brake bike as the donor chassis, we added front caliper brakes for safety. An engine cover, engine-stop button on the handlebars, and speedometer finished it off.

The finished product. Gary's engine cover produced in ABS was a tough, fuel-resistant protective finishing touch. It carried the winged Zipcycle logo.

The final design was a well-handling motorized bicycle that the average rider would have no difficulty in riding or controlling. We had multiple riders try out the bike –from older riders who had not ridden in years to enthusiasts who rode daily. The unanimous verdict was a crazy grin when they returned from a test ride. One pivotal reason was the total weight added was only 11 pounds and the additional weight was balanced in the center of the frame triangle, so the motorized version rode and handled as easily as a regular bicycle. It was exactly like riding a bike with a magic "push" all the time, sort of like coasting downhill all the time. If one wished they could travel by pedals as long or as far as they wished and then motor back home. On down hills I would often stop the engine, pull in the clutch, and coast silently down the hill and part way up the next, releasing the clutch to engage the engine when needed. I did feel the experience offered the best of both worlds, both pedal and powered.

TECHNICAL DETAILS

Since we had an extensive background in building CNC machines (3-axis wood routers) which ran almost completely by toothed drive belts, we chose this method to transmit the torque from the engine to the friction drive roller. The system of driving by a toothed belt is durable, quiet, and forgiving of slight misalignments. We removed the original Homelite string trimmer flexible shaft (along with the pull-start mechanism and the original flywheel cover) and replaced it with a toothed-belt drive gear, then by a Kevlar belt to the rear drive roller. We were concerned initially by the fact that we had introduced an additional side thrust to the crank bearing, but we ran extensive tests and never lost an output bearing. (The Homelite engine design utilizes two large ball bearings on the power output side.)

Because the original flywheel cover and subsequent cooling airflow had been modified, we pushed the engine to its limits to ascertain the cooling capabilities of the engine. We found the engines could be run wide-open on the bench for a complete tank of gas and not overheat. At the same time, we had a wonderful test track in back of our shop so that many, many miles were put on the bikes. One bike, "Old Red", was ridden daily for almost a year by the partners and the part time workers to test out modifications to the drive train. We found that one roller would last about as long

A line up of finished bikes awaiting shipment. These appear to be the lowest-price version known as the "Sportsman". Lighter in weight, they did not have fenders or the added tank. The drive unit was the same as all the other gasoline bikes.

Most of the advertising featured more "mature" couples, since the majority of buyers were in this age bracket.

as three rear tires, which were much cheaper to replace. Since there was virtually no slipping, we did not notice any appreciable rear tire wear.

The bike was pedal-started. To crank the engine, the rider pulled the clutch lever (swiveling the engine upward and moving the drive roller down away from the rear tire), and began pedaling. Once balanced, the rider released the clutch lever and pushed slightly on the start lever, which pushed the roller into contact with the tire. As the engine fired, the direction of the drive roller caused it to "over-center cam" into the rear tire. The rotation of the engine mount caused the drive roller to press deeper into the tire as the rider increased the power. We found a necessity was to keep at least 45 pounds of air pressure in the rear tire. To stop, the rider simply squeezed the clutch lever, which disengaged the drive roller, and braked to a stop. The engine continued to run. To start again, the rider assisted the bike at the start, and then smoothly engaged the drive roller.

Gary designed an engine cover and created an original mold, so we had a friend create a multiple die for a vacuum molding supplier to volume-produce ABS engine covers. At the same time I transferred all the engine mount and drive train blueprints to CAD files and we contracted with a laser-cutting company to produce the engine mounts. We hand-built the first 20 or so bikes (all after 8:00 PM and a full day's work at the regular career) and then hired a couple of part time students to assemble the bikes. We sold them mostly on the Internet and through ads in *Walneck's Cycle Trader*.

We were concerned with the legalities of riding a Zipcycle, so I made an extensive Internet survey of state laws concerning motorized bicycles and found that they were covered under state laws concerned with the operation of mopeds. I was given valuable assistance in this area by several moped clubs. The majority of states considered that a motorized bicycle with less than two horsepower and still capable of being pedaled was, for their purposes, either a bicycle or a moped. This meant that license, registration, and the mandatory helmet restrictions that applied to motorcycles did not apply to motorized bicycles. Some states restricted the use of motorized bicycles to persons 16 or older, and some states specifically specified that moped engines must be less than 50cc. Since motorized bicycles were considered just a bicycle and thus unable to maintain 55 mpg, all states barred them from the interstate highways.

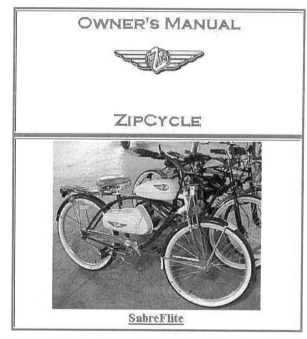

But the Zipcycle was legal in virtually all states, subject to local ordinances. The legal situation was clearer in states that had specific moped laws, and less clear in states that did not specifically delineate mopeds. I remember speaking to one dealer from North Carolina and he referred to the Zipcycle as a "DUI-cycle" and I replied that I was unfamiliar with the term. He explained that persons who had lost their driver's license due to liquor violations in his state were reduced to riding a bicycle to get back and forth from work. But since motorized bicycles did not require a driver's license, he was selling them as basic transportation for those affected.

Our owner surveys revealed that the vast majority of purchasers were mature riders who were either motorbike enthusiasts or nostalgia fanatics. Since we were both, we understood our niche market and worked to keep the appearance of the Zipcycle to the "retro" style. Most of our purchasers rode them in parks, campgrounds, and retirement villages. I do not believe that younger riders were ever attracted to the Zipcycle, preferring instead 4-wheelers or minibikes.

By 1998 we were running ads in national magazines. The phone was starting to ring.

In 1999 we were contacted by a group of local businessmen about the possibility of investing in our operation. One of them, Neal Shipman, was an old friend of long acquaintance. Neal had put together several successful companies and was looking for an additional challenge. He was interested in taking the Zipcycle nationwide, so he put together a group to purchase a majority interest in the company. Gary and I stayed on as advisors and minority stockholders.

Neal's group added much-needed capital and moved the manufacturing operation from our small machine shop to a much larger facility which was renovated to become an ideal motorized bicycle manufacturing plant. Neal convinced his son Eddy, a graduate mechanical engineer, to come with the company as chief engineer and designer. Eddy had an extensive background in designing and building his own motor vehicles, computer-assisted-design, and manufacturing. Within a short time Eddy worked miracles, getting the empty plant ready for production, training new employees, getting the production line up and running, and began producing 20 to 30 Zipcycles per week. He also started designing a newer, smaller Zipcycle based on a 20" bicycle frame. At the same time Neal instituted a nation-wide advertising campaign, advertising mostly in magazines and at the same time began developing a dealer organization. Brochures were printed, dealers were signed up, a web site was created, and the Zipcycle saga began.

In response to dealer requests, Eddy added an electric bike to the mix. Since his research time was being taken up with his many other projects, he chose to go with a developed electric package offered by Curry Technologies, Inc. Our company, now named Micro-Power, purchased the electric kits and installed them on standard bicycle frames. The kits proved to be a reliable developed design that offered a good alternative for those who wished a quieter ride. We put the electric bike to many tests and it passed them all with flying colors.

Sales were mostly in the southern states with retirement areas and tourist areas predominating, but some sales went abroad to Japan, Switzerland, and South America. A dealer organization began to build as Micro-Power showed its products in national bicycle and motorcycle shows. Fortunately, one of the investors was a local attorney, Scott Shipman, so we

CHAPTER 7

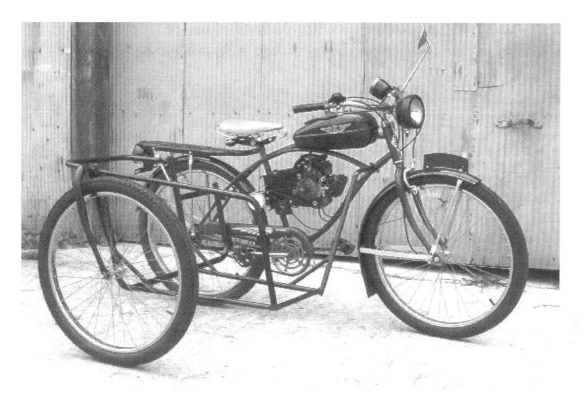

Many variations of the Zipcycle were created. This work-in-progress was destined to become a sidecar version. The body is yet to be added to the sidecar frame.

With tongue firmly in cheek we called this stretched lowrider version "The Hardley-Ableson".

profited by having a seasoned group of company directors who wisely guided the infant organization through the early days of establishing a going business.

By 2001, the company was steadily producing, selling and shipping about 20 to 25 bikes a week and looking forward to their first year of producing over 1,000 Zipcycles a year. More different products were added to the lineup. One in particular, a lowrider on a stretched cruiser frame, gained the name "The Hardley-Ableson" and generated intense dealer interest. Sales were naturally higher in the summer and at Christmas time, so the plant used the slacker times to build inventory for the busy seasons and develop new designs.

Changes in the Bicycle Industry

Over the years of Zipcycle production, the engine supplier, Homelite, (which was sold at least three times, including once to John Deere) altered the plastic housing and fuel tank, but thankfully never changed the standard aluminum cylinder-head and block castings, so our engine mounts were able to remain basically the same. In the first year of production we continued to purchase new Homelite string trimmers in bulk as donors for the engines, discarding the trimmer head and engine cover. But as we ramped up production for the second year, I contacted the Homelite organization about purchasing just the bare engines. Although the company officials were very cordial, they explained that in order to make the changes to produce a bare engine with their highly automated production facilities, they would need a minimum order of 10,000 engines to start. So we continued to purchase the whole string trimmer and strip off the parts we didn't need (we eventually filled a warehouse full of string trimmer extensions, covers, and heads). We seriously investigated several other brand small engines that could be purchased alone, especially 4-stroke ones, to see if there were any advantages. After trying several, we found that the original choice of Homelite seemed to be the best all-around candidate.

The little Homelite engine was a sturdy and reliable workhorse. It started easily, usually on the first try if the push-bulb primer was used. It did not overheat and withstood an occasional over-rev on downhill runs. With more than 2,500 Zipcycles produced we only had to replace one engine, and I am certain that in that case the owner had neglected to add oil to the gasoline supply. We replaced the engine without comment in order to maintain relations with a good dealer, but added a large bright red warning tag about the necessity of adding oil to every gas tank cap after that.

Zipcycle purchased the Currie Technologies electric kits in bulk and installed them on our regular bike chassis. They were very reliable.

What changed was the bicycle industry. In a period of less than seven years the entire bicycle production left the United States to foreign manufacturers. We started out purchasing bare bikes directly from the Murray factory in Lawrenceburg, TN in the 1990s and we were satisfied with the quality and lower shipping costs. But Murray, along with all the other volume producers, could not compete with the foreign imports. In an effort to reduce costs, Murray shut down their bicycle manufacturing operations at their Lawrenceburg, TN plant and established a non-union assembly plant in Mississippi, basically bringing in welded and painted frames from abroad and assembling the rest of the bike there. Again, we continued to use Murray bare bicycles and continued Zipcycle production using Murray bikes made in Mississippi. But after producing bikes for a couple of years in Mississippi, Murray was still unable to compete with the low labor costs of the foreign bicycle manufacturers. Finally, Murray (along with Huffy and most others) ceased all US production. To tide the plant over, the company directors made the decision to purchase the entire remaining inventory of the closed Murray plant, giving the young company the needed time to find other suppliers. Warehouses were rented to store the remaining inventory.

Then the Zipcycle management team looked at the investment required to purchase bikes in bulk from China. The minimum purchases were container-sized loads, payable in advance. In addition to this capital requirement, a continuing challenge to the company officials was the yearly re-negotiation of liability insurance. Zipcycle had found that most dealers and re-sellers of our products required proof up-front of a large liability coverage in case of lawsuits. Zipcycle also found the word "motorized" makes most insurance agents run for the back door. Although Zipcycle never had one single lawsuit, the best terms for product liability that could be negotiated added approximately 30 to 40 dollars per unit to the cost of every Zipcycle.

But still the team soldiered on, selling, building and shipping motorized bicycles and building inventory for a great Christmas for 2001. The events of September 11, 2001 changed everything. The phone stopped ringing; dealers stopped re-ordering and Christmas came and went with no splurge of orders like the previous year. Because Zipcycle had an excellent management team and virtually no indebtedness (other than its obligations to its stockholders), it was able to continue on for another two years of decreased sales. But the boom days never came back and so after multiple tries at different promotional ideas, the management team made the unhappy decision to cut their losses and close the plant. The exact number of motorized bicycles produced was a little hazy, but probably just in excess of 3,000. This is counting the electric bicycles, but the vast majority of the sales were the string-trimmer powered classic bicycles.

Another interior shot of the factory with rows of crated bicycles stored on shelves awaiting assembly and engine installation.

This motorized bike was built from magazine-supplied plans. Note that the frame had to be modified to fit in the early Briggs & Stratton engine.

This is my "tribute" to the classic board track racer. I reinforced the fork and stretched the frame of a regular cruiser bike and added a China engine modified with a "faux" crankcase. The set-back seat and fabricated wheel stand complete the look.

Chapter Eight

Roll Your Own

No book about motorized bicycles would be complete without a section that deals with attempts to build a powered bicycle out of materials already on hand. Although it may seem daunting, the fact is that thousands have accomplished this and some have gone on to publish plans and some (like us) have gone on to produce a manufactured kit. At the start I must qualify the following by stating up front that this section is not for technically advanced with a home workshop that looks like a machine shop or for those with unlimited budgets or those who wish to set a new land speed record. Rather, it is for those who wish to consider an inexpensive project made from materials around the house (or local building supply or auto part shops).

How much power does it really take?
The answer is—surprisingly little. Part of the success of motorizing bicycles is the little known fact that very little power is actually needed to propel a single rider down the road, especially if you are planning to assist the bicycle in starting by pedaling. The best indicator of how much actual power is needed is the power output of the average bicyclist. Calibrated studies by the Human Powered Vehicle Association have shown that the average healthy human can produce about ½ horsepower in a short burst and about 0.2 to 0.3 horsepower continuously. Of course, world-class competitors like Lance Armstrong can produce much more, up to 0.4 to 0.5 horsepower for 8 hours. But we do not need this much just to cruise

12 to 14 miles per hour on level ground and pedal power can always be added to help on the hills.

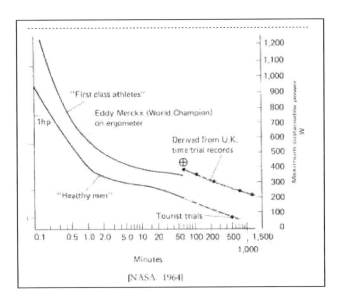

Note: approx. 760 Watts equals about 1 horsepower. Most bike riders are putting out less than one-third horsepower.

Higher speeds, of course, do require much more power for the average rider on a bicycle does not present an aerodynamic shape. The power needed to travel faster than 20 to 25 miles per hour increases dramatically because of the rapid increase in wind drag. The basic equation for calculating the drag caused by aerodynamic forces reveals that to double the speed, one must quadruple the horsepower. But speeds in excess of 20 miles per hour on a regular bicycle are not recommended. The regular bike frame is not constructed to combat such stresses and the regular (non-disk braked) bicycle brakes are not designed to provide such stopping power. For these speeds you need a motorcycle with drum or disk brakes, a heavy-duty frame, and a helmet.

Consider a Kit

The quickest way to a motorized bicycle, of course, is to purchase and install one of the dozens of kits available today. The advantages of this approach are many; the proven nature of a well-developed package, the engineering built into the kit, and the speed of installation. Most of the kits on the market today can be installed within one weekend and one can be out riding the next week. With most kits, an owners group is in existence and madly emailing each other on the Internet about the pros and cons of their particular choice. Now with the wide spread network of forums on the 'net, knowledge about any one kit can quickly be obtained. Most kit manufacturers are advertisers on the motorized bicycle forums so if very many purchasers are unhappy about the delivery, service, or reliability of the kit, you can bet they will be posting on that forum.

Power Sources

In the past, the two most popular sources of power to motorize a bicycle were cast-off lawn mower, tiller, and washing machine engines. Of these, the ubiquitous small side-shaft Briggs & Stratton was the most popular, mostly because so many were made and available to back-yard mechanics. Besides Briggs & Stratton, other sources were the small air-cooled engines made by Clinton, Tecumseh, Wisconsin, Kohler, Lauson and others. The little Maytag washing machine motor was also popular back in the thirties and forties, mostly for the same reason. As electrical power was extended to the farms and byways, the little engines were discarded and replaced with electric motors. Both the single cylinder and the twin cylinder Maytags were popular sources for motorizing bicycles and other small vehicles. Some handyman magazines even published articles with specific instructions on how to convert a used lawnmower engine to power a bicycle.

Similar to the one used on the Zipcycle, cast-off string-trimmer engines or small chain saw engines can also be adapted. They are mostly of

CHAPTER 8

the two-stroke variety, but these types of engines have multiple advantages; they are lighter in weight, less complex, physically smaller, and generally cost less. Invariably, most cast-off engines are not worn out, but simply failed to start due to something simple such as a clogged carburetor a fouled spark plug. Once the original owner jerks the pull cord until he is out of breath, his next thought is probably to trash the device and buy another, all the while muttering something about the poor product quality. When faced with an engine that has suddenly fail to start, the very first thing a small engine repair shop does is to: (1). Put in fresh gas and insure it is getting to the engine, and (2) Pull the spark plug and make sure it is getting a hot spark. By the way, the best source of cheap engines for such a project as this is the local small engine repair shop. He will have dozens of engines that are not worn out and offer many more years of service.

This small engine from Harbor Freight is often offered for less than $100.00 (less shipping)

It seems that lately the choice of small, inexpensive air-cooled engines has greatly increased, mostly, I suppose, because of the Internet. But some large chains such as Harbor Freight and Tractor Supply are now offering small 1-3 horsepower engines at a low price. When they have a sale (as Harbor Freight often does), the price of the engine (not counting freight) often drops below $100.00. So many builders have taken advantage of the Harbor Freight engine that the engine is known on the discussion boards as the "HF" engine.

This automotive blower motor is cheap and runs on 12 volts.

And gasoline engines are not the only power source. Consider building an electric powered bicycle. Small electric motors are abundant and cheap, if not free. It is possible to build a low-buck ebike from parts found around the house. A good source of small powerful 12-volt electric motors is automobile blower motors.

Since most of these will be brushed motors, they will not have the highest efficiency rating, but most are very efficient when compared with gasoline engines. Most junk yards have blower motors by the dozens but you may be required to take them off yourself. The best part is they are all designed to run on 12 volts. The power generated by most blower motors will be adequate for most riders on most terrain. Again, for the hills or to instantly accelerate the rider could always just kick in some pedal power.

In the last few years there have been large advances in brushless motor power and efficiency, but all of these types require a separate controller and the price climbs accordingly. In the same manner, batteries are in the process of evolving in efficiency and storage, but the price also climbs accordingly. If you are interested in maximum efficiency (or range) there are multiple forums on the Internet dealing with DIY electric bicycles (and scooters).

Sealed Lead-Acid batteries such as these never need re-filling and can be used in any position.

For batteries there are now multiple choices. The optimal inexpensive battery would be something like the Sealed-Lead-Acid (SLA) motorcycle battery. These are widely available and very reasonable in price. Of course there are the higher energy density batteries such as the Lithium-Ion types, but they come with a much higher price and most home builders are looking for the cheapest solution.

Applying the power to the wheel

Once the choice (whatever is lying around the house) of powerplant is made, the next most important choice is the method chosen to send the output of the engine to the driving wheel. This is the most complicated part of motorizing a bicycle and the point where most failed efforts occur. Don't dismiss the fact that the simplest and easiest method of applying power to a wheel is by means of a friction drive. There are drawbacks, of course, but this method eliminates gears, sprockets, and chains and the associated complications of providing the correct gear ratio. This is why some of the most successful aftermarket bicycle drive kits have friction drive ones. The down side of friction drive is slippage in wet conditions. The reality is that very few people deliberately go out bike riding in the rain. However, some wish to use their motorized bike to commute to work or others need to travel, even in the rain. For these, it should be kept in mind that the normal pedal system should still work and could be used at any time. Most friction drive users have found that although the system does have a slight tendency to slip in wet conditions, the effect can be minimized by judiciously applying power and adjusting the drive roller tightly against the tire. This is why the most successful friction drive kits have some sort of abrasive drive roller and a method of adjusting the pressure between the drive roller and the bicycle tire.

The friction drive setup similar to the one pictured just below is easy to install and maintain. This one is a police bike fitted with an electric friction drive kit from Zap Systems.

This is a home-built motorized bike using a Briggs & Stratton engine driving the rear wheel by means of a belt. The tank looks like it came from a Whizzer.

The simplest bicycle engine is a friction drive unit that fits over the rear wheel.

Installed in a road bike, the China engine is small enough to fit within the frame triangle and geared just right to drive a regular bicycle.

The China engine incorporates a cable-operated clutch and an internal gear reduction to make it suitable to drive a bicycle.

CHAPTER 9

Chapter Nine

The Import Explosion of China Engines

Just after the millennium year 2000 two trends intersected to radically re-introduce the motorized bicycle to the world public. The first trend was the increasing ubiquity of the Internet and the increasing popularity of Internet forums and Yahoo! Groups. As the forums increased in number and in membership, several were dedicated to members motorizing their own bicycles. These members were not interested in factory-built motorbikes or mopeds, although they may have owned one or two, but consisted of individuals wishing to combine the best qualities of a bicycle with the best qualities of an internal combustion engine. These were do-it-yourselfers who wished to roll their own. As the forum members posted their experiences and photos and as they swapped ideas and dreams, a consensus seemed to emerge that building your own motorized bike from scratch was not only doable, but being done daily. The forums doubled their size monthly in membership and member posts.

At the same time, small economical 2-stroke engines imported from China that were ideally suitable for motorizing a bicycle began to emerge on the market, especially on eBay. Most of these were included in a kit that comprised the engine, gas tank, chain and sprocket, and controls and cables to completely motorize a bicycle in a weekend or so. By the year 2005, prices on the kits had fallen to just below $200.00 and the sales skyrocketed. Dozens of importers offered kits and the price competition was murderous.

Of course the forums fanned the flames and discussed the pros and cons of each importer, but along the way the barrage of stories and pictures of completed projects caused many to leap into the building mode. There were precautionary tales of fried engines, missing parts, and dishonest dealers, but in the main most builders reported successful results and happy grins as they rode their motorized bicycles.

The right side view of the engine

A large part of the success for most builders rested in the design of the power unit most commonly offered on the Internet. The engine itself was a 2-cycle that was narrow enough to fit between the bicycle pedal arms and small enough to fit within the center triangle of most full-sized bicycles. Most of these Chinese import engines appeared to be virtually identical with only minor variations in trim or finish. The engines varied from 49 cc. to 66 cc. and all contained a built-in gear reduction drive output of about 18 to 1. This gear reduction allowed the little engine to rev to its peak performance of about 6,000, affording a road speed of 25-35 miles per hour. The single-gear reduction drive incorporated a cable-operated dry clutch, allowing the engine to maintain an idle at stops without having to re-start the engine.

But just as important was another feature of the design which was the power transmission from the engine to the rear wheel. As designed, virtually all the kits utilized a chain drive from the engine to the right side (the normal bicycle chain on the left side was left untouched) of the rear wheel. At the rear, a sprocket was provided that bolted on the bicycle spokes with rubber dampening. No jack shaft, no other gears, sprockets, idlers, or transmissions. Just a simple chain driving a sprocket on the right side of the rear wheel.

The bicycle frame remained unmolested with no welding or drilling to weaken the tubing or cause problems later on. The engine was secured to the frame by clamps that bolted on the down tubes. The gas tank supplied bolted on to the top tube, the one that runs from the steering tube back to the seat. The kit could fit most common-sized bicycles, but fit most readily on the older, classic cruiser frames. It could be adapted to fit most (non-suspended) mountain bikes and road bikes.

The engines were ideally suited for the regular cruiser frame.

It could be transferred from one bicycle to another—just not very quickly—if the owner wished to change to another style. For builders who admired the old board-track racer style of bicycle, the little engines were a natural; they allowed the builder wide latitude in engine placement and drive train details. Most builders reported good results with their kit within two weekends or so. A few suffered from broken spokes and everyone learned to use some form of threadlocker to keep nuts from loosening on the high-revving engine.

To add to the advantages of the kits, virtually all the Chinese import engines have the same carburetor mount, so replacement carbs could be purchased if needed. Likewise the solid-state firing system seems to be a standard design, so replacements were plentiful and cheap. Suppliers of these replacement parts offered their wares on the Internet and on eBay.

The clone engine drove the rear wheel by a chain. A sprocket was added to the rear wheel.

Component manufacturers leaped on the bandwagon and quickly offered different sized rear sprockets—some optimized for top speed and others geared for stump-climbing ability. Different type and capacity gas tanks were offered, while add-on lighting systems were next to be added. As the number of kits grew, several start-up companies began to offer multi-speed gearboxes and variable speed drive units. The kit manufacturers responded with pull-start options and additional electrical capacity in order to power a lighting system.

This is the contents of the most popular version of the clone engine kits. It contains everything (except common tools) needed to convert your bicycle to a motorized one.

One of the basic criticisms of the clone engine was its two-stroke nature. This type of engine requires mixing oil in the gasoline prior to using and many find this unhandy or tedious. Others are turned off by the fact that if the amount of oil is not carefully regulated, the engines are prone to emit smoke. The two stroke fans maintain that this type of engine is lighter, less expensive to manufacture, and easier to repair if anything goes wrong. Furthermore, they point out that new smokeless oils are available to eliminate the problem of smoking.

The growth in popularity of YouTube only fanned the flames of motorized biking. As members posted their short videos of building and then riding their completed vehicles, the possibilities of successful building seemed more and more achievable. The amazing growth of two of the motorized bike forums on the Internet (one has over 10,000 members, the other over 26,000 members!) are an indication of the popularity of motorized biking today.

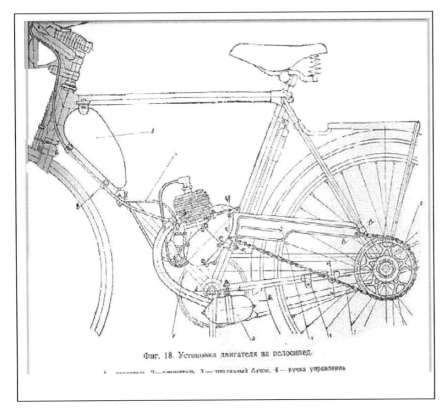

This is a page from a Russian Type "D" Owner's Manual from the 1950s. Note that the engine appears identical to the later Chinese clone below. Only the placement of the gas tank is different. The drive chain and rear sprocket on the right side are similar. See the sidebar on the following page.

The placement, engine layout, and drive system are virtually identical with the earlier Russian one show above. But the millions produced in Russia distilled a better solution to motorizing a bicycle. The evolved versions are more reliable and less expensive.

The Russian Type "D" Bicycle Engine

     The most common engine used by most motorized bicycle builders today seems to be produced in multiple factories located in mainland China. They all have a family resemblance if not almost interchangeable parts. The carburetors, ignition systems, and exhaust systems are a standard configuration and can be swapped with engines from other suppliers. How did the design get to be so widespread and how did it get developed? These questions are not easily answered given the nature of today's off-shore clone manufacturers, but the answer seems to start in Russia during the fifties and sixties.

     The design seems to have been an evolved edition of a Russian 2-stroke commonly known as the Type "D" engine made for Russian mopeds back in the fifties. One widespread story has the engine being developed in an aircraft factory that needed additional products as the Cold War began to wind down. Even then the engine was available in 40cc, 50cc, and 60cc options. According to some sources, the engine was initially offered in a 50cc. version in 1956 and by 1974 over 5,000,000 copies had been produced! In Russia the engines are still known as the "D" engine, and they were still being produced in the 1980s.

     Photos of the Type "D" engine from the 50s produced in Russia share many similarities with the present-day Chinese clones. Of special note is the identical nature of the internal gear reduction, the enclosed dry clutch, and the chain power takeoff arrangement. Even the crankcase castings are virtually the same. It is clear that the engine was designed (or developed) to drive a bicycle or moped, since the output gear ratio is ideal for driving a 24" to 26" wheel.

     Regardless of the exact origin of the design, it is clear that many, many copies of the earlier design abound today in Russia, still driving mopeds and motorized bicycles. No information exists on how the design traveled to China, but once it did, and once the engine kits appeared in the U.S., sales took off. Soon the engine was being offered by multiple importers and appeared in greater and greater numbers on websites and eBay. Today, the entire kit can be purchased for just over $100.00.

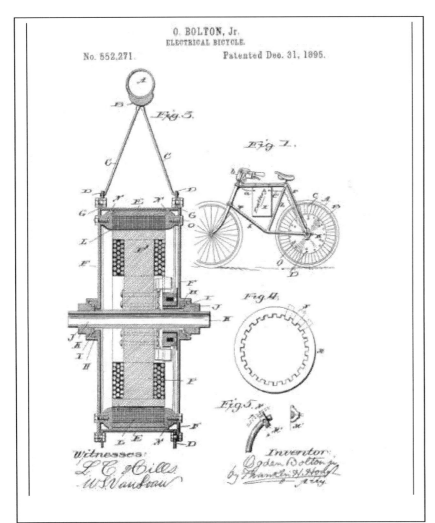

Electric bicycles were being invented just as the bicycle itself was coming on the market. The technology of the battery did not keep up with the electric motor technology, however.

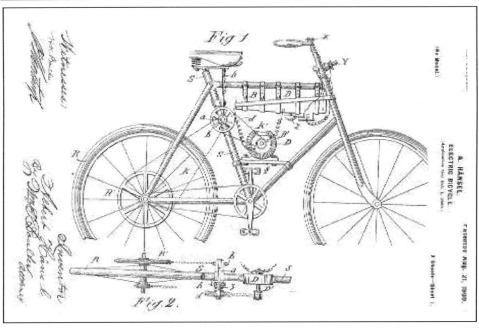

Albert Hansel realized that the motor could act as a brake and a generator also.

Chapter Ten

The Electric Powered Bicycle

Early efforts by inventors to motorize a bicycle by the addition of an electric motor paralleled the efforts to add an internal combustion engine. Even before the turn of the century, electric motor-powered bicycles were the subject of applications for U.S. patents. As early as 31 December 1895 Ogden Bolton Jr. was granted U.S. Patent 552, 271 for a battery-powered bicycle with "6-pole brush-and-commutator direct current (DC) hub motor mounted in the rear wheel." There were no gears and the motor could draw up to 100 ampere from a 10-Volt battery. Bolton's invention would have required the bicycle owner to swap out the original rear wheel with the one containing the hub motor. But to control the motor speed, Bolton simply connected a single battery via a rheostat. This method offers a smooth increase in current, but herein resides a major problem with most of the earlier electric bicycles. A rheostat controls the current supplied to the electric motor by means of a coiled resistance wire. The current that is not fed to the motor is wasted as heat given off by the rheostat. All this heat is, of course, wasted battery power. It could be argued that this waste process takes place only when the bicycle is being accelerated from a stop and that at high speed all the battery current is fed to the motor, but this acceleration occurs every time the bicycle is stopped. Not until the advent of modern true solid-state electronics did the electric bicycle get beyond the wasteful rheostat to control speed. Given the limited nature of the early electric batteries it is understandable that all earlier electrically powered bicycles suffered from a range that was too short.

Two years later, in 1897, Hosea W. Libbey of Boston was granted a patent for his design of an electric motor powered bicycle (U.S. Patent 596,272) that was propelled by a "double electric motor." The motor was designed to fit within the hub of the crankshaft axle. Still again a year later in 1898 Mathew J. Steffens patented a rear wheel drive electric bicycle which transferred the power from the electric motor by a belt that ran to a sheave around the outer rim of the rear wheel.

And the following year U.S. Patent 627,066 was granted to John Schnepf, who used a rear wheel friction "roller-wheel" to drive his electric bicycle. But an important statement was noted in Schnepf's patent. Schnepf observed that if the unit was left turned on and in physical contact with the wheel while going down a hill, the motor would act as a generator and the resulting current could used for charging: *"...if the rider encounters a decline, the motor may be thrown into contact with the driving-wheel J and utilized as a dynamo to recharge the battery."* Schnepf's observation would become very important 85 years later in the future development of electric bicycles.

In a patent granted by the United States Patent Office in 1900 (patent # 656,323), Albert Hansel, a citizen of Zeitz, Germany, took this concept one step further. He realized that the battery could be recharged anytime the rider desired to slow down by *"employing the electric motor as a brake...whereby the storage battery will be (re-) charged."* This was possibly the first American patent to specifically recognize the concept of regenerative braking for an electric bicycle. Regardless of the precise origins, it is clear that not only were electric bicycles being built by the turn of the century, but also that the principle of regenerative braking had been recognized and patented. But the power available from a gasoline internal combustion engine was so much greater that the electric powered bicycle, for the most part, languished for nearly a century.

The modern electric "hub" motor driven bicycle was described in the 1939 patent #2,179,418 granted to Thomas M. McDonald of St. Ignatius, MT. McDonald's electric hub motor used a ring gear to transmit torque to the wheel rim through the wheel spokes. Although McDonald's hub motor depicted driving the bicycle through the front wheel, it could also power the bike through the rear.

With the rapid increase in petroleum prices in the 1970s, innovators and entrepreneurs looked again at the electric bicycle. One of the earliest producer of electric bicycle motors in the 1990s was ZAP (Zero Air Pollution) out of California, but their electric bicycle motor kit relied more upon massive advertising than on high technology. A simple friction drive kit, the brushed electric motor gave good service and quite a few were sold. But the future of electric bicycles needed to take advantage of the solid-state revolution and soon products began to appear that did just that.

One of the first to fully utilize solid-state switching technology with a modern electric motor was Dr. Malcolm Currie, co-founder of Currie Technologies, a major producer of electric bicycle kits and completed electric bicycles. Currie was the former chairman and CEO of Hughes Aircraft and Delco Electronics where he led major developments in defense, electronics, satellite communications and automotive electronics. Currie and his staff combined the latest technology in low-loss switching with a high-efficiency brushless motor to produce what was arguably the most advanced electric bicycle motor at that time. In 1998 Currie first discussed his developments of an advanced electric bicycle motor to the Schwinn Company but nothing really resulted from the discussions. Currie then went on to market and manufacture electric bicycle motor kits. His efficient design was able to extract the maximum distance from the batteries that were currently offered and the motors proved to be reliable. Zipcycle used his designs and found them to be largely trouble-free and a very good experience to the rider.

The Currie System used electronic switching to add power smoothly. It was a very reliable unit.

No discussion of electrically powered bicycles would be complete without a mention of the story of the **EV Global** electric bicycle and Lee Iacocca, Jr. Iacocca, the reputed "father" of the Ford Mustang and the savior of Chrysler back in the 1980s, was looking for another challenge after retiring for the second time. Too restless to really enjoy retirement, Iacocca continued to search among transportation alternatives for a more economical solution. He suspected he might have stumbled upon the answer in teaming up with the Giant Manufacturing Company of Taiwan.

Giant had been making and importing bicycles to the United States for several years and was a major player in import bikes. They felt the market was ready for an electric bicycle and so they designed one and looked about for a major player with a higher profile. They certainly found one in Iacocca. Reportedly, he was so taken with their design that he invested $600,000.00 of his own money in the creation of EV Global Motors and drew no salary at the first. Iacocca's expertise was in setting up automobile dealerships and initially this is the way he first marketed the electric bikes. The first shipment of bikes was made in March of 1999. Disappointed with the slow sales, Iacocca moved to add independent bike shops as part of the distribution network.

Iacocca was hoping for sales of 50,000 **E-Bikes** for the first year through the combination of bike shops and auto dealers. There were several models of his electric bike, which was equipped with a 35-pound, removable battery, and featured a top speed of 18 – 20 mph and a maximum range of approximately 16 miles. The battery used was the conventional lead-acid battery found in many other applications. The selling price was approximately $1,200. Iacocca's name certainly brought recognition to the new electric bicycle. He appeared on network television shows in the morning and the late night talk shows afterward.

Iacocca's E-bike was a tested design, only a little bit heavy…too heavy to pedal any distance.

By the time a year had passed, EV Global had sold only 12,000 e-bikes, far less than Iacocca's earlier hopes. Apparently the company had not made any money on the bikes that it did sell. By 2001 Iacocca's company, EV Global, had emerged as the leading seller of **electric bikes** in the United States, outselling such competitors as Giant Bicycle and Currie, but it still did not even approach the number of sales that Iacocca and the company founders felt were possible.

Finally admitting that he had been unable to generate the sales of electric bicycles that he had envisioned, Iacocca moved on to the next big thing. Today EV Global bikes can still be found on eBay and Craig's list, mostly needing a battery replacement, but were well-designed and tested electric bikes, if a little heavy.

Another entrant in the electric bicycle business from the motor city of Detroit was the Ford Motor Company. In the late 1990s the CEO of Ford Motor Company, Jac Nasser was looking toward the future of the transportation business. He was concerned about recent legislation in the state of California that mandated a small shift toward zero-emission vehicles. At that time the only technology that would satisfy the mandates were all powered by electric motors. Nasser led the company to purchase a Norwegian company, THINK, that produced a series of battery-powered bicycles and golf-cart sized vehicles. The THINK brand was to be a brand name within Ford Motor Company and would encompass any alternatives (including fuel cell technology) within that brand. When it was purchased, the THINK technology was a point of national pride in Norway.

The Ford THINK bikes were introduced in January, 2000 in two different versions; a THINK bike "Fun" model with a rigid frame and regular bicycle pedals with the option of power assisted pedaling, and the THINK " Mobility" with a similar drive train but with a foldable frame. Both bikes were powered by 400 watt electric motors driven by 24-volt batteries. The top speed of both bikes was about 16 miles per hour and their range varied from 18 to 20 miles.

Unfortunately, the THINK electric bikes sales were harmed by problems and recalls in the THINK electric cars. Plagued by poor sales and recalls, Nasser and Ford decided to discontinue the entire line in 2002. Ford divested itself of the THINK stock but the resulting company, Think Global, continues to produce electric cars in Norway

The Ford THINK bike had a radical appearance, not at all like a regular bicycle. Pedaling it very far could be very fatiguing.

Half way around the world a massive revolution was beginning to take place in electric powered bicycles. The center of the revolution was in China. There, the sales of electric bicycles have zoomed from 40,000 in 1998 to 10 million in 2005! This last number may be slightly misleading, for it combines the sales of electric bicycles with the sales of electric scooters. This combination is because in many cases the electric scooter also has pedals to satisfy legal restrictions, but no one is seriously using the pedals. But the technology behind both types of electric vehicles is similar.

Virtually all of the electric two wheelers in China are driven by a hub motor, solid state controller, and rechargeable battery. The electric bicycles typically have 36 volt motors and lighter batteries while the electric scooters typically have 48 volt motors and larger batteries in order to carry more cargo (or an extra person). In most Chinese cities electric bikes may use the regular bicycle lane and are not registered as a motor vehicle, therefore no license or helmet is required. The electric scooters, however, must be licensed, tagged, and driven in the normal traffic lanes. Both are equipped to be able to be recharged by a regular electrical outlet, so many are being charged in the daytime at the workplace while at other times recharging is taking place at night to take advantage of lower electrical rates.

Building the electric motor into the front (or rear) wheel hub enormously simplifies the drive system. No additional chains, belts, or pulleys. Just a rotating armature that turns the front wheel.

The reasons for this dramatic surge in the adoption of the electric bicycle in China are complex; it has taken place in three stages of growth. The first stage started in the 1960s when consumer demand started growing. As China began to industrialize, the need for more transportation alternatives became apparent but factories were still unable to meet the consumer demand. Electric bicycles began to appear but most people were unaware of their abilities and could only afford a regular bicycle. However, annual sales reached only 10,000 to 20,000 per year due to competition with the inexpensive gasoline engine scooters.

The second stage was reached in the late 1980s when the government began to demand more energy efficiency. Again, the electric bicycles were compared with the small gasoline powered scooters and again failed to gain significant market share against the competition.

The third and crucial stage started in 1991 when the Chinese National Science Board named the electric bicycle, or e-bike, as one of the top 10 technology goals for the next 5-year plan. In 1993 Shanghai founded the Electric Vehicle Industrialization Center as some cities, choked with pollution, began to consider the banning of gasoline powered scooters in the downtown districts. In 1995 Shanghai suspended the licensing of gasoline scooters and other cities began to follow. In 1996 the first National Forum on e-bikes was held as most large cities began to adopt restrictive regulations on gasoline powered vehicles in their city centers.

In the year 2000 the National Department of Traffic Control drafted a "Road Transportation Safety Law" to allow e-bikes to use bike lanes as long as they retained the pedal feature and restricted speeds to below 20 kilometers per hour (about 12.5 mph). In 2003 the widespread severe acute respiratory syndrome (SARS) outbreak caused many Chinese to avoid the public transportation system and sales of e-bikes soar as a result of workers seeking alternative transportation. By 2005 the annual sales of e-Bikes topped 10 million electrically powered bicycles. In 1998 only 10 original equipment manufacturers (OEMs) were listed, but by 2005 the number had grown to 481 and the 6 largest producers were putting out over 200,000 e-bikes each.

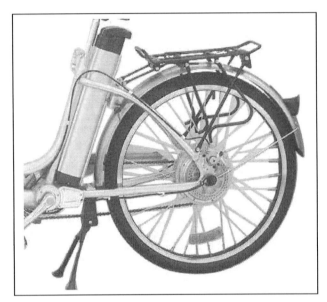

This Chinese eBike has the electric motor built into the rear hub and the battery carried beneath the seat. Note the tail light for safety.

A large part of the growth in the public acceptance of the e-bikes came from two technical advances in electric bicycles; the first part came from the advances in lead-acid battery technology. Although the lead-acid battery had been around before the turn of the century, it historically suffered from a short life span of recharge cycles. That is, the earlier lead-acid batteries became useless after 100-120 recharge cycles and had to be replaced. Advances in battery life led to batteries having at least 300 recharge cycles before having to be replaced. At the same time, battery manufacturers replaced the liquid electrolyte (which could be spilled if the battery was upset) with fixed electrolyte that was sealed from the factory. The batteries were safer, longer lasting, and needed no maintenance, other than recharging. As the price continues to drop on other types of batteries possessing a higher energy density such as NiCad, NiMH, and Li-Ion batteries, the traditional lead-acid battery may finally be replaced by another type.

Next was the introduction of brushless motor technology into electric bicycles. Previous to this time, manufacturers had used the simpler brushed motors that were less expensive but inherently less efficient. In the early 2000s, many e-bike makers switched to brushless hub motors. At the same time the manufacturers were able to increase the motor efficiency from about 60% to slightly better than 85%, giving a much better range than previous motors. All these factors resulted in the widespread adoption of the e-bike as a major transportation avenue in China.

Just like the Moped in Europe, Chinese eBike designs are departing from the traditional triangle frame bicycle shapes to stamped metal step-through designs.

As with any new technology, different variations of electric propulsion are offered for bicycles. One variation that is gaining in popularity is the hybrid assist electric, in which the electric motor assists the rider who must continue to pedal. This type offers an extended range since the battery drain is not as much as a fully powered one. In Europe, this type is termed the "Pedelec" and utilizes a torque sensor to add power to the input from the rider. This power can be used to assist in climbing hills or increasing in speed. Some countries call this an "assist" motor and allow the bike on bike lanes, but specifically exclude gasoline engine powered bicycle from their bike lanes.

MOTORIZED BICYCLES

Chapter 10

Appendix A: Motorized Bicycle Forums, Websites, and Groups

www. Motoredbikes.com: Founded in late 2006, this forum was one of the first Internet forums to specialize in motorized bicycles. As of the date of this publication, it has slightly over 10,000 members with over 1,000 members who post regularly. The forum lists over 230,000 posts on 22,500 threads. A great resource of information and history of motorized bicycles.

www.Motorbicycling.com: Founded in late 2007, this forum grew even faster, topping 26,500 members. It currently lists slightly over 200,000 posts on 18,000 threads. Both of these forums are a goldmine of photos of finished projects, precautionary tales, and general inspiration.

www.lst1090.org/scooter: This website actually includes motorized bicycles, motorscooters and minibikes. It is well-organized and has a short illustrated history on most of the motorbikes and scooters manufactured in the United States, with a few European and Asian manufacturers listed. A very helpful feature of this website is the "Information Wanted" and "What is it?" sections.

www.users.globalnet.co.uk/~pattle/nacc/arcindex: Better known as the Moped Archive, this British site now contains over 900 articles about cyclemotors, autocycles, mopeds, and motorized bicycles. Although it necessarily devotes much of the site to British and European makes, the American manufacturers are well represented, especially the earlier ones. The site is particularly well organized and clearly presented.

w*ww*. www.ebikehub.com: Although both of the above forums include a section just for people interested in converting their bicycle to an electric-powered one, this web forum specializes in electric bicycles only. Lots of good information for those who are mechanically inclined but need to brush up on their electronic skills.

www.bikeforums.net: Most bicycle forums are now beginning to accept electric bicycles as a legitimate part of their sport. This forum not only accepts members with an interest in electrifying their bike, they set aside a separate section for swapping information on the process.

MOTORIZED BICYCLES

Index
Italicized entries refer to Illustrations

Allis-Chalmers Co., 19
Anzani Cycle Motor, 27
Anzani, Alessandro Ambrogio, 26
AquaBug Bicycle Motor, 45
AquaBug, 46
Armstrong, Lance, 65
Auto Cycle Union, 23
Automotive Hall of Fame, 16
Benz, Karl, 5
Bicycling Hall of Fame, 10
Bike Bug Bicycle Motor, 45
Bike-Bug engine, 47
Birch, Frank, 12
Bleriot, Louis, 26
Bockscar, 42
Bolton, Ogden, Jr., 77
Boneshaker, 3
Breene-Taylor Engineering, 30
Breene-Taylor, 30-32
Briggs & Stratton Co., 16, 17, 66
Briggs & Stratton Motor Wheel, 17
Briggs & Stratton powered bicycle, 69
Briggs, Stephen, 17, 21
British Petroleum, 51
Brushless hub motors, 81
BSA motorcycle, 13, 26
Bugatti cyclemotor, 27
Bugatti, Ettore, 27
Buzz-Bee Bicycle Motor, 46
CDI ignition, 37
Chevrolet, 34
Chicken Power, 43, 45
China engine, 70
Chinese National Science Board, 81

Clement Bicycle Motor Kit, 11
Cleveland Welding, 33
Clinton engine, 66
Copeland, Lucius Day, 5
Coventry-Eagle Autocycle, 25
Cucciolo "Little Puppy", 51
Cucciolo, 51
Currie, Dr. Malcolm, 78
Curry Technologies, 60, 78
CVT, 38
Cyc-Auto Autocycle, 24
Cyc-Auto, 22, 24
Daimler, Adolf, 6
Daimler, Gottlieb, 5
Daimler, Paul, 6
Dandy horse, 2
Davidson, Arthur, 9
Davis Sewing Machine Co., 18
Dayton Bicycles, 18
Dayton Motor Bicycle, 12, 18
Delco Electronics, 78
Department of Transportation, 37
Draisene, 2
Ducati, 51
Dunlop, John Boyd, 4, 7
DynaCycle, 42
DynaCycle, 43
eBay, 71
Einspur, 6
EV Global, 78-80
Evinrude, Ralph, 21
Excelsior (American) Motorcycles, 8, 10
Excelsior (British), 24
Excelsior autocycle, 25

Excelsior Supply Co., 10
Farinelli, Aldo, 51
Ford Model T, 13
Ford Motor Co., 16, 80
Ford Mustang, 78
Francis-Barnett Autocycle, 25
Free Spirit Bicycle Motor, 45
Giant Manufacturing Co., 78
Goldman, Martin, 31
Gorman, George H., 18
Goudard, Maurice, 49-50
Guinness Book of World Records, 16
Hansel, Albert, 78
Harbor Freight engine, 67
Hardley-Ableson, 61
Harley Davidson Motorcycles, 9-11
Harley, William S, 9
Harley-Davidson, 19
Hedstrom, Oscar, 7-9
Heintz, Ralph M., 40
Hendee Mfg. Co, 19
Hendee, George M., 7, 19
High Wheeler, 3
Hildebrand & Wulfmuller motorcycle, 6
Hildebrand-Wulfmuller, 6
Hobby horse, 2
Homelite String Trimmer, 54
Homelite, 53-55, 62
Honda Moped, 53
Honda, 45
Hudson Hornet, 34
Huffman Mfg. Co., 18
Huffman, George, 18
Hughes Aircraft, 78
Human Powered Vehicle Association, 65
Iacocca, Lee Jr., 79
Indian Bicycles, 7
Indian Motocycles, 8

Indian Motorcycle, 19
Jack & Heintz Co., 40
Jack & Heintz, 40
Jack, William S., 40
James Autocycle, 25
James Autocycle, 25
James Cycle Company, 25
James, Harry, 25
Jawa Babetta, 53
Jefferson, Thomas, 1
John Schnepf, John , 78
Johnson Brothers, 20-21, 40
Johnson Outboard, 21
Johnson Outboard, 21
Johnson Twin Motor Wheel, 12. 20-21
Kohler engine, 37, 66
Kohlsatt, Dietrich, 31
Lallement, Pierre, 2-3, 10
Lauson engine, 66
Lead-acid batteries, 81
Leoni, Aldo, 51
Libbey, Hosea W., 77
Li-ion battery, 81
Marman Clamp, 42
Marman Products Co., 41
Marman Twin, 42
Marsden, John, 24
Marx Brothers, 41
Marx, Herbert "Zeppo", 41
Maybach, Paul, 5
Maytag engine, 66
McDonald, Thomas M., 78
Mechanix Illustrated Magazine, 43
Mennesson, Marcel Patent, 48
Mennesson, Marcel, 49-50
Merkel Motor Wheel, 19, 21
Merkel, Joseph, 19
Michaux, Pierre, 2-3

Michelin, Andre, 4
Michigan Agricultural College, 19
Micro-Power, 60
Mikuni, 37
Millet Steam Bicycle, vi
Mobylette, 50
Motobecane, 50-51
Motorrad, 7
Murray Corp., 62-63
NASCAR, 34
Nasser, Jac, 80
New Departure, 33
New Hudson Autocycle, 25-26
New Hudson Autocycle, 26
NiCad battery, 81
Nielsen, Harald, 52
NiMH battery, 81
Norman Autocycle, 25
O & R Engines, 43-45
Oak Ridge National Laboratories, 42
Ohlsson & Rice, 43
Ohlsson, Irving, 43-44
Otto, Nicholas, 5
Outboard Marine Corp. (OMC), 21
Pedelec, 83
Perks, Edwin, 12
Perreaux, L.G. ,4
Peugeot Bima, 50
Peugeot, 50
Piggins, Vince, 34
Pope Manufacturing Co., 4, 10
Popular Mechanics Magazine, 43
Power Bike by Saginaw Products, 47
Pratt & Whitney, 24
Puch Maxi, 52
Raynal, 24
Rice, Harry, 43-45
Roadmaster bicycle, 33

Roberts, Bruce, 30
ROC motorcycle, 13
Rogers, Gary, 53-54
Roosevelt, Franklin D., 31
Roper Steam Powered Bicycle, vi
Roper, Sylvester, 4, 11
Roxbury, MA, 4
Rudge Autocycle, 25
Rudge Cycle Co., 25
Rudge-Whitworth, Ltd., 25
Russian Moped engine, 74
Safety bicycle, 3, 6
Schuricht, Henry, 31-35
Schwinn Bicycle Co., 10
Schwinn, 34
Sealed Lead Acid (SLA) batteries, 68
Sears & Roebuck, 45
Sears Mo-Ped, 53
Shaw Mfg. Co., 13
Shaw, Stanley, 13
Shipman, Eddy, 60-63
Shipman, Neal, 60
Shipman, Scott, 60
Simplex (British), 27
Singer Bicycle Company, 12
Singer Company, 18
Singer Motorized Three Wheeler, 13
Smith Flyer, 16
Smith Motor Wheel, 15, 16
Smith Motor Wheel, 19
Smith, A.O., 15-16
Smith, L.R., 15-16
Smithsonian, 5
Solex, 44, 49
Solexine, 51
Starley, Joseph, 3, 6
Steyr-Puch, 52
Sturmey-Archer, 34

Suvega Moped, 50
Tanaka Bicycle Motor, 45
Tanaka Engines, 45
TAS Spitz Bicycle Motor, 45-46
Tecumseh engine, 66
THINK electric bike, 80
Thomas, Frank, 42
Three Spires Autocycle, 25
Tillotson carburetor, 33
Type "D" moped engine, 75
Velosolex, 50
Velosolex, 51-52
Vespa Ciao Porter, 52
Victory Motors, 20
Villiers Cycle Components Co., 24
Villiers engine, 25, 26
Villiers Junior Engine, 22, 24
Von Drais, Karl, 2

Wall Auto Wheel, 19
Wall Motor Wheel, 13, 14
Wall, William Arthur, 13
Walneck's Cycle Trader, 59
War Production Board, 31
Whitworth Cycle Co., 25
Whizzer Engine Patent, 28
Whizzer models,
Whizzer Motor Company, 32-38, 40
Whizzer motorbike, 29-39, 42, 43, 53
Whizzer motorbike, 28, 30-32, 34-35, 36, 38
Wilson Foundry & Machine, 33
Wisconsin engine, 66
Wolfmuller, Alois, 7
Yahoo!, 71
You-Tube, 73
ZAP Power Systems, 68, 78
Zipcycle, 53, 55, 58, 61, 63

Made in the USA
Lexington, KY
23 June 2016